D

AMERICAN AUTHORS AND CRITICS SERIES

GENERAL EDITOR
JOHN MAHONEY
University of Detroit

JAMES FENIMORE COOPER
PORTRAIT BY JOHN WESLEY JARVIS ABOUT 1822

JAMES
FENIMORE
COOPER

An Introduction and Interpretation

WARREN S. WALKER

Texas Technological College

HOLT, RINEHART AND WINSTON, INC.

New York • Chicago • San Francisco • Toronto • London

ABOUT THE AUTHOR

WARREN S. WALKER teaches at Texas Technological College. He was Fulbright Lecturer in American Literature at Ankara University, Turkey, 1961-1962. In addition to numerous articles published in professional journals, his writing and editing include *Nigerian Folk Tales* (with Barbara K. Walker), *Twentieth-Century Short Story Explications, Leatherstocking and the Critics, Tales Alive in Turkey* (with Ahmet E. Uysal), and introductions for Cooper's *The Spy, The Red Rover,* and *The Sea Lions.*

PREFACE

My special acknowledgments are due to Professor Emeritus Harold W. Thompson of Cornell University, under whose direction my study of Cooper was begun; and to my wife, Barbara K. Walker, through whose patient assistance this work was brought to completion.

I also wish to express appreciation to Miss Patricia Harris of Barnes & Noble for her many helpful suggestions in the preparation of the final draft.

Many thanks are given the New York State Historical Association at Cooperstown, especially Miss Ruby M. Rounds and Mr. Frederick L. Rath, Jr., for helping us secure a number of the illustrations used in this book. Appreciation is also expressed to Mr. Paul Fenimore Cooper of Cooperstown, who gave us permission to use Susan Cooper's crayon drawing of the Cooper children.

To Benjamin Weintroub and *The Chicago Jewish Forum* and to Charles Wallis and the *New York Folklore Quarterly* appreciation is expressed for permission to reprint material previously appearing in article form and now included in Chapter 3 of this book. Grateful acknowledgment is also made to J. M. Dent & Sons, Ltd., for permission to reprint a passage from Joseph Conrad's *Notes on Life and Letters* (1921) and to Random House, Inc., for permission to quote from William Faulkner's *Requiem for a Nun*, copyrighted 1931, 1950, and 1951.

Although Otsego Hall is no longer standing, Cooperstown on Otsego Lake is now the site of three museums sponsored by the New York State Historical Association and offers much Cooperiana and Americana, as well as scenic beauty, to the visitor.

W. S. W.

CONTENTS

ILLUSTRATIONS

CHARTS

CHRONOLOGY

1789   James Cooper, born on September 15 at Burlington, New Jersey, to William and Elizabeth (née Fenimore) Cooper.

1790   Moved with family to Cooperstown, New York, the village founded by and named for his father on Otsego Lake, the source of the Susquehanna River.

1801   Entered the preparatory school kept by Reverend Thomas Ellison, an Episcopal clergyman, at Albany, New York.

1803   Entered Yale College.

1805   Expelled from Yale after perpetrating several pranks.

1806   Sent to sea as a common sailor before the mast for a voyage to London and the Mediterranean on the merchant ship *Stirling*.

1808   Issued a midshipman's warrant in the United States Navy on January 1.

1809   Inherited $50,000 at the death of his father, who was fatally injured by an assassin while leaving a political meeting.

1810   Took furlough from Navy, to which he never returned for active duty.

1811   Married, on January 1, Susan DeLancey, daughter of wealthy landowners in Westchester County, New York.

1817   After six years of shuttling back and forth between Westchester and Otsego Counties, settled at Scarsdale and started construction of a home at Angevine Farm, on DeLancey lands.

1819   Became head of the entire Cooper clan after the death of the last of his five elder brothers; assumed full responsibility for Cooper estates now heavily in debt.

1820   Published his first book, *Precaution*, a society novel of the type then current in England; it was unsuccessful.

1821   Published *The Spy*, the first significant American novel and one highly praised by nearly all reviewers.

1822   Moved with his growing family to New York City.

1823   Published *The Pioneers,* the first of the *Leather-Stocking Tales;* his son Fenimore died; his household goods were seized by a sheriff at the behest of creditors but not sold.

1824   Published *The Pilot,* the first of his eleven tales of the sea.

1826   Continued the Leather-Stocking series with *The Last of the Mohicans;* added *Fenimore* to his name to keep alive his mother's family name; sailed for Europe after large testimonial dinner sponsored by The Bread and Cheese club of New York City and attended by a host of celebrities from the East Coast.

1826–1828   Lived at Paris, into whose society he was introduced by the Marquis de Lafayette and the Princess Galitzin; published *The Prairie* while there.

1828   Published, in London, *Notions of the Americans,* a book that offended both British and American critics; started, with his family, on Grand Tour of the Continent that carried him through France, Switzerland, Italy, and Germany.

1830–1833   Lived at Paris, where he became involved in French politics while assisting Lafayette; wrote *Letter to General Lafayette* for the Finance Controversy, a project which earned him unpopularity at home.

1833   Returned to America to find himself unwelcome in New York City; promptly left there to live again at Cooperstown.

1838   Presented the public with a defense of his Jeffersonian political and social philosophy in *The American Democrat* and two novels, *Homeward Bound* and *Home as Found.*

1839   Published his definitive *The History of the Navy of the United States of America* in two volumes.

1840   Published *The Pathfinder* in the Leather-Stocking series.

1841   Published *The Deerslayer,* the final volume in the Leather-Stocking series.

1842   Won judgments against both Thurlow Weed and Horace Greeley in two of the many libel suits he brought against newspapers during the last years of his life.

1843   Edited the autobiography of an old shipmate from the *Stirling,* Edward Myers, with whom he was reunited after more than thirty years: *Ned Myers, or a Life Before the Mast.*

1845–1846 Published a fictional trilogy, *Satanstoe, The Chainbearer,* and *The Redskins,* in defense of the landlords' position in the Anti-Rent Wars in New York State.

1850 Published his last novel, *The Ways of the Hour.*

1851 Died on September 14, one day before his sixty-second birthday, at Cooperstown.

1852 Memorial services held in February in New York City, presided over by Daniel Webster; letters read from Hawthorne, Melville, Emerson, Longfellow, and others; William Cullen Bryant read a memorable and perceptive tribute, "Discourse on the Life, Genius, and Writings of James Fenimore Cooper."

Now, here am I, a hunter and a scout and a guide, although I do not own a foot of land on 'arth, yet do I enjoy and possess more than the great Albany Patroon. With the heavens over my head to keep me in mind of the last great hunt, and the dried leaves beneath my feet, I tramp over the ground as freely as if I was its lord and owner; and what more need heart desire?

—*Leather-Stocking*

1

ᵃᶻ THE SQUIRE'S SON

WHEN William Cooper moved his large family from Burlington, New Jersey, to the shores of Otsego Lake, central
New York was still frontier territory. The power of the Iroquois
Confederacy had been broken by then, but the wilderness was still
to be tamed; civilization was yet to be established. No one was
more aware of this than was James's mother, who refused to stir
from her armchair as the Cooper caravan was ready to forsake
the comforts of city life for the formidable forests that lay at the
headwaters of the Susquehanna; and no one was more determined
to accept the challenge of the wilderness than was William Cooper,
James's father, who hoisted his wife, armchair and all, into the
lead wagon and pointed the horses' heads toward the north. The
year was 1790, and James (not yet Fenimore), the youngest of
seven children on the trip, five others having died in infancy, was
only thirteen months old.

The wagon train came to a halt weeks later at the southern end
of Otsego Lake, destined to become the Glimmerglass of the
Leather-Stocking Tales and site of the fictional town of Templeton. Here William Cooper had already begun, on occasional visits,
to clear a section of the vast tract of land, more than half a mil-

lion acres, that he and a partner had bought on speculation during the closing days of the Revolution, and here a frontier village had been founded, Cooperstown. (Thus the town is named not after James Fenimore Cooper, as many suppose, but after his pioneer father.)

William Cooper, a descendant of English Quakers, was a remarkable man, and from the day he took up permanent residence here at the source of the Susquehanna River, the whole surrounding area began to stabilize and flourish. He rode to its crest the wave of prosperity that he himself had started, but he had earned the eminence he soon enjoyed. He was appointed to a local judgeship, elected twice to a seat in the House as a Federalist Congressman, and deferred to by local and national leaders as a major political power in New York State west of the Hudson River. His success, both as a politician and as a frontier patriarch, lay, to a great extent, in his understanding of the common man, an intuitive shrewdness in human relations that seldom failed. Unlike so many of the great landowners in the state—the Van Rensselaers, the Livingstons, the Schuylers—Judge Cooper avoided the temptation of renting his holdings with perpetual leases, but rather sold them outright, in fee simple, with long-term mortgages that rode lightly on the shoulders of the already encumbered pioneer settlers. Nothing, he believed, so readily flatters human dignity or promotes individual industry as the ownership of land. And when the day of reckoning came in the 1840's with the bloody struggle in New York State between landlords and tenants, none of the battles of the Anti-Rent War was fought on Cooper lands. In all, he settled over 40,000 people before his death in 1809, and his posthumous pamphlet *A Guide in the Wilderness* (1810) became a handbook for frontier leaders.

In his daily contacts with old neighbors and new settlers, the Judge was always a hail fellow, never "above his business," as the local saying had it. Whenever the community pooled its manpower to raise a barn, seine the lake, or clear a piece of public land, he rolled up his sleeves and promptly joined the laborers. With his ready example and timely encouragement much of the public construction and maintenance in Otsego County was willingly undertaken by the resident landowners. "A few quarts of liquor cheerfully bestowed," he wrote, "will open a road or build a bridge which would cost, if done by contract, hundreds of dollars." He won friends and votes with a year-round campaign of folksiness and benevolence. And he often won over even his enemies by settling his differences with them in wrestling matches, drinks for all present to be bought by the loser. The robust and manly paternal image in several of Cooper's novels derives largely from the qualities of William Cooper.

Tangible evidence of the Coopers' success was their impressive brick mansion, Otsego Hall, and it was here that James Cooper lived during most of his boyhood. He wanted for nothing by way of physical comforts, and his mother, who detested the frontier, saw to it that the children were introduced to as many cultural refinements as she could have brought overland from Albany, Philadelphia, and New York City. What absorbed young James more than books and music, however, lay beyond the drawing room. By the time he was nine he had already formed a Wordsworthian attachment to forest and lake that was to last the rest of his life; by the time he was twelve he was beginning to be aware of the pageantry of frontier America.

Cooperstown, accessible by river and lake, was strategically located, and in 1790 it was to be thirty years before the bulk of pioneer traffic would take a more northerly route along the Erie Canal. Through the new village passed European immigrants newly arrived and Yankees who had finally forsaken their boulder-strewn acres for the rich river bottoms waiting in the Midwest. There was in the air of the place a sense of national destiny. At the Hall James could observe the passing parade of dignitaries— statesmen, military leaders, land investors—who conferred continually with the old Judge. At the store the daily conversation that he heard often turned upon land claims, road and bridge building, the construction of grist and saw mills, commerce with eastern cities, the fostering of local industries for producing lye and maple sugar, and the function of the State in supporting the struggling settlements. Then again, the talk might devolve to the passing and petty animosities that split the town between Federalists and Republicans, between Anglicans and Presbyterians, or between resident New Yorkers and the itinerant Yankees who were invading the state from the east in alarming numbers. Here was a microcosm of the American frontier, with all its promise and all its problems, at the end of the eighteenth century. How much of it was impressed upon the sensibility of the boy would be attested later by more than a dozen novels, including the ever popular Leather-Stocking series.

❧ ❧

James received his elementary education at the local "academy" at Cooperstown, except for two winters when he attended school in Burlington, the place to which his mother, rather quixotically, still hoped to maneuver the family again. In 1801 he was sent to a preparatory school run by the Reverend Mr. William Ellison in his home, the rectory of St. Peter's Church in Albany. It was an exclusive group of young gentlemen whom the Episcopal divine taught there, among them two Van Rensselaers, a Jay, and a Livingston; and the curriculum was weighted heavily toward the classics, especially Vergil. The son of an Englishman and himself an alumnus of an English university, Ellison annoyed young Cooper with his sense of British superiority, his carping antirepublicanism, and his frequent humor at the expense of the boy's idol, the recently elected President, Thomas Jefferson. But whatever differences there may have been between student and mentor were ended peacefully by the untimely death of the Rector in April, 1802. And so, more than two years ahead of the schedule laid out carefully by the Judge for the boy's education, James headed for New Haven, there to receive special tutoring to ready him for admission to Yale College.

He entered Yale early in 1803, thirteen years of age and only two weeks older than the youngest student there, the future poet James A. Hillhouse. Cooper was "a fine, sparkling, beautiful boy," one of his professors was later to recall, a boy "of alluring person and interesting manners." Unfortunately, this favorable impression that he made upon his arrival was not the one he left in the minds of the faculty when he was expelled two years later. Younger than his peers, Cooper was not immediately taken into their group; more advanced than they in his understanding of the Latin language and its literature, he was not challenged by his courses; and free at last from the rather strict supervision of his father and of William Ellison, who had acted *in loco parentis,* he was not inclined to submit willingly to any new authority. It was an inauspicious beginning for a college career. He wasted his time, dawdled with his studies, ran up substantial debts in fashionable shops in town, and eventually directed his ample energies to the

4

Watercolor by Freeman, 1816

ELIZABETH FENIMORE COOPER, COOPER'S MOTHER, IN OTSEGO HALL, COOPERSTOWN perpetration of campus pranks. One escapade led to another: a brawl of donnybrook proportions, a donkey taught to sit in a professor's chair, and finally a classmate's door blown open with a charge of gunpowder. Even William Cooper's great influence could not now forestall the inevitable any longer, and so in the summer of 1805 James was expelled and sent home to Cooperstown in disgrace.

The old Judge was not amused. James was the second son to be expelled from college, William Jr. having been recently dismissed from Princeton for similar misconduct. Was he overindulging his boys, he wondered, spoiling them with paternal kindness, perhaps even setting in motion the proverbial three-generation progress from shirtsleeves to shirtsleeves? As time was to prove, he was, in fact, doing just that, for James's five brothers were to squander their fortunes, dissipate recklessly, and die in middle age —none lived to be forty-five—leaving their families unprovided for and, in some instances, all but destitute. This fate for the house of Cooper the Judge could only fear and fight against at the time, but the blow he struck against it saved his sixth son, James, who eventually recouped both family fortune and reputation. The Judge sent the boy to sea in October of 1806, an ordinary seaman before the mast.

The move was only partly punitive, however. His decision was certainly dictated as much by shrewdness as by indignation. The Judge foresaw clearly the necessary growth of the American Navy —he himself had been one of its leading advocates in Congress— and he was mindful of the opportunities it might hold for a young man with the right connections. That many younger sons of wealthy English families had risen to eminence through the rigging of a man-of-war he well knew. And thus, as he replanned the activities of this son just rusticated from Yale, he decided to launch him upon a naval career. To take the initial step of securing a midshipman's warrant, in those days before the Academy at Annapolis, a young man had to log some actual experience at sea. It was with this goal in mind that William Cooper made arrangements with Captain John Johnson to take his son aboard the *Stirling,* a small merchantman bound out of New York with a cargo of flour, for a voyage to England and Spain.

James Cooper's boyhood days in and out of Cooperstown came to an end that fall when he went down to the sea for his boot

6

training. He was not to renew permanent residence in Otsego County for more than twenty-five years, a quarter of a century during which he made literary history, enjoyed the subsequent fame, and came to know the fragility of "the bubble reputation."

◅§ ৪▻

James's tour of duty on the *Stirling* was a rude awakening to the rigors of life that lay beyond the sanctuary of the squire's peaceful domain. The account of his experiences and impressions, patched together from comments by Cooper himself and from the reminiscences of his shipmate Ned Myers, reads like a story of initiation. The crew that shipped aboard the *Stirling* was probably standard for the period: the flotsam and jetsam of society, derelicts and drunkards, Ishmaels, and a few old salts with hearts of oak and a love of the deep; these were the men, some of them ill after their fling ashore, some of them in *delirium tremens*, whom the young Cooper, just barely seventeen, joined for his first voyage. After a stormy crossing, they were pursued off the coast of Portugal by a pirate ship, an armed felucca that dogged their wake for days. "A stern chase is a long chase," an old seaman observed to Cooper, and the *Stirling* managed to reach British waters before the freebooter could overtake her. But the safety afforded there turned out to be only relative, for they were promptly boarded by a recruiting party from one of His Majesty's cruisers. The War of 1812 was yet to be fought, and the impressment of American seamen into British naval service was a common occurrence. The *Stirling* lost several able-bodied seamen before it landed in England and still more during its stay at London. Even Captain Johnson, rigged in the disguise of a country squire, could not elude the Admiralty's agents, and he was held captive by a shanghai team for several hours until he could have his papers brought from the *Stirling* to prove his identity. "Them press gang chaps smelt the tar in his very boots," the mate remarked later.

It was nearly a year before the *Stirling* re-entered New York harbor, time enough for Cooper to learn the ropes, mature considerably, and adjust to the demands of shipboard discipline. He was now qualified for the midshipman's warrant that he received, signed by Thomas Jefferson, on January 1, 1808, and he reported with high hopes for his first assignment in the Navy the following month. It turned out to be a grave disappointment. Eager for duty on a capital ship, Cooper found himself attached instead to a lowly bomb ketch—worse yet, an inactive bomb ketch, the *Vesuvius*, laid up for repairs in New York City. And his dreams of romantic voyaging to exotic lands faded completely when, a few months later, he was transferred inland two hundred miles from the sea to Oswego, New York, a frontier village of twenty-five loghouses on the shore of Lake Ontario. His duty there was to aid in the building of a small American fleet to counter the growing British naval power on the Great Lakes. He was assigned to the staff of Lt. Melanchthon Woolsey in command of this outpost where a 240-ton brig-of-war, the *Oneida,* was under construction. It was a dreary, isolated place—"this *sickly* country," Cooper described it in a letter home—and the naval officers joined forces with officers of a detachment of the Sixth Infantry stationed nearby to relieve the monotony with a series of social events, including a cotillion attended by a number of the local ladies, some of whom came barefoot!

Still, time hung heavy on their hands, and they snatched at any prospect of deliverance. "The rumour of War [with France] is strong," Cooper wrote to his brother Richard in November, 1808. "If the latter should be true, adieu to Lake Ontario. I shall have the pleasure of seeing salt water once more." But the rumor was false, the winter came and went, and by spring Cooper was becoming desperate. He wrote to the Secretary of the Navy requesting a transfer. He pleaded with his superior officer for more active duty, and Woolsey, sympathetic with the young midshipman, first recommended him for promotion, and then, to flatter his ego, left him in charge of the post for two months. This mollified him for the moment, but the prospect of wintering again at Oswego was too much, and Cooper was determined to escape. He wrote to the Secretary again, this time requesting a furlough for the purpose of taking a voyage to Europe on a merchantman; officers commonly did this at a time when the tiny Navy of only twelve first-class ships could not provide them all with sea duty. The furlough was granted, and Cooper went to New York City, supposedly to find a berth on an outbound ship. But this was not his real intention at all, for he immediately proceeded to pull strings to have himself attached to the *Wasp,* an 18-gun sloop at anchor there, a beautiful, trim vessel commanded by James

("Don't give up the ship!") Lawrence. In haste, he wrote once more to the Secretary:

> I have the Honor to state to you that having arrived here in pursuance of a Furlough from the Navy Department for purpose of making an European voyage; the difficulty of procuring a berth on board of any ship bound to Europe as well as the advice of several officers of rank in the navy, have induced me to relinquish the idea—
>
> Capt. Lawrence of the *Wasp* has been so obliging as to inform me that he would receive me on board his ship. I therefore take the liberty to request that I may be attached to that vessel—

The request was approved, he reported to Lawrence, and at last his ocean dreams seemed about to materialize, only to fade away once more from his view. Ironically, Lawrence thought him such a personable young sailor that he appointed him the *Wasp*'s recruiting officer with shore duty in New York City! It is possible that Cooper was aboard the sloop when, in March, 1810, she made a four-day cruise to Boston on a recruiting mission, and if so, it was his only salt-water voyage with the U. S. Navy while he was on active duty.

The sea was Cooper's first love, but fate conspired at every turn to keep them apart; in the spring of 1810, however, he courted another. In New York City he had met Susan DeLancey, daughter of a well-to-do Westchester County family. Descended from a Huguenot ancestor who settled in America in the seventeenth century, the DeLanceys had, at an early date, become solidly established, related by marriage to several prominent New York families—the Van Cortlandts, the Heathcotes, and the Schuylers among them—but their family star went into eclipse during the Revolution when they espoused the Loyalist cause in the Colonies and subsequently lost much of their property by the Confiscation Act of 1777. They had managed to retain enough, however, so that even in Susan's day Cooper could describe them in a letter home as having "respectable connections and a handsome fortune." In May of 1810 Cooper requested a year's leave to attend, he said, to some of the affairs of the family left unsettled after the death of his father in December 1809; the Judge had been struck from behind when leaving a heated political meeting at Lewis Tavern in Albany, and he had died of the complications that resulted. It was the probing of his own heart rather than of his father's will, however, that moved Cooper to go on furlough, and he spent the rest of that year courting Susan, then eighteen, "amiable, sweet-tempered, and happy in her disposition." They were married at her home in Mamaroneck on January 1, 1811, though only after she had been persuaded that he had forsaken the sea and he had "made a pledge to resign" from the Navy.

But who can so order the ways of the heart? Cooper only thought that he could forget the sea, little knowing that it was to call to him—and he to answer—for the rest of his life. When traveling, whether at home or abroad, he never passed up the opportunity to go by water. His European travel books of later years abound with descriptions, often chapter length, of those hours of his journeys spent at sea, and occasionally the nautical details are so technical that the reader might forget that Cooper was a passenger and not the captain. In 1829, for example, he described with delight a trip down the length of Italy from Leghorn to Naples in a small coaster, a thirty-ton felucca. At Vevey he rented a sailboat for an entire stay in Switzerland and spent countless hours adrift on the mountain-rimmed waters of Lake Geneva. Back in Cooperstown after returning from Europe Cooper kept a yawl on Otsego Lake, and when Ned Myers visited him there in 1843, the two former shipmates sailed up and down the reaches of the lake trading yarns and recalling their youthful escapades aboard the *Stirling*. He sailed with other old comrades, too. Friends in the Navy, many of whom became ranking members of the service, made it possible for him to keep his sea legs with their invitations to inspections and cruises aboard American men-of-war. In 1842, to cite but one such lark, he was treated by Commodore William Shubrick, a fellow midshipman of thirty-odd years earlier, to a twelve-day voyage on the U.S.S. *Macedonian*.

Perhaps the closest he ever came, after his marriage, to answering again the call of the running tide was in 1819 when he bought a two-thirds interest in the whaler *Union*. On the surface it was a business enterprise, but underneath the cash and collateral burned the old love, that flame that family and duties ashore could never extinguish. For the next three years, whenever the *Union* was in her home port of Sag Harbor, Cooper dropped everything he was doing and hastened out across Long Island to take charge of her.

He sailed her about in the coastal waters and insisted on over-seeing personally the refitting that was necessary for the next voyage to the whaling grounds. Apparently her skipper, Captain Jonathan Osborne, had poor luck too often in the chase, for she did not always return with a hold full of oil, and Cooper's purse could not afford to indulge indefinitely his feelings in the matter. Sometime in the early 1820's he was forced to relinquish his share in the ship, but the experience left him with a wealth of recollections which he salted down for the future.

Short of being afloat, the next best thing, of course, was to live close to the water where one could hear the crash of the waves and sniff the freshening breeze. Whenever Cooper chose a residence, whether for only a few days or for a longer stay, he almost always managed to find a good view of the water. This was true of all his temporary homes in Europe; it was true of Angevine Farm at the DeLancey holdings in Westchester; and so, too, with Fenimore Farm on which he retired at Cooperstown. Before Thoreau said it, Cooper knew that "It is well to have some water in your neighborhood to give buoyancy to and float the earth. . . ."

⊷§ ৡ⊶

For ten years after his marriage Cooper gave little promise of greatness. With neither training for a profession nor any inclination for business, he had no immediate prospect for a career following his resignation from the Navy. He shuttled back and forth between the Cooper estate in Otsego County and that of the De-Lanceys in Westchester, building comfortable homes at both places, but coming to rest, for the time being, at the latter in 1817, the year of his mother's death. There he farmed, speculated in the land market, and joined all the local organizations on the side of the angels: the Westchester County Agricultural Society, the Westchester County Bible Society—he had been one of the founders of the American Bible Society in 1816—and the Clintonian Republicans, the dominant political party. Dependent, as he was, partly on the favor of his in-laws and partly on the inclinations of his elder brothers who stood between him and the Cooper inheritance, his position was equivocal. The decade following his marriage was one of the few times in his life when he was so pressed financially that money was his major preoccupation.

At the death of William Cooper each of his sons had inherited

$50,000 plus succession, by seniority, to the Cooper estate, which had a total value of over $700,000. Not accustomed to frugality, they spent the cash freely, and depended for the future on the income of their patrimony. But gardens must be cultivated if they are to produce, and Cooper's brothers were hopelessly inept at their tillage. Actually they never tried very hard. Reared to be gentlemen, they did not deign to put their hands to the plough, and under their mismanagement the estate yielded little. Their one recourse, to stall off ruin by selling their acreage piecemeal, was frustrated by the recession after the War of 1812 which deflated land values sharply. Debt-encumbered and defeated, Cooper's five brothers all died between 1813 and 1819.

Cooper now became the *pater familias* with the responsibility for providing, somehow, for all of his brothers' many dependents. He borrowed when he had to, he reorganized both the Cooper and the DeLancey farms, he invested speculatively—even his interest in the whaleship *Union*, at this time, being rationalized as a profitable venture. Despite his valiant efforts, however, it is doubtful that he would have survived had it not been for the success of his final and seemingly least practical venture of all, the writing of novels.

According to family tradition, Cooper's first novel was written on a dare. Supposedly, in the customary practice of the day he was reading aloud to his wife one evening from a current English novel, but found the story dull. Throwing it aside, he declared, "I could write you a better book than that myself." And Susan's challenge to make good his boast resulted in his writing *Precaution* (1820), an all-too-typical novel of the period, set in England, peopled with English characters, and filled with the oozy sentimentalism in which the contemporary female audience loved to wallow. There is good evidence that *Precaution* was influenced to a slight degree by Jane Austen's work, and Cooper cultists have offered endless speculation on whether it was an Austen production that Cooper bragged he could excel, and if so, which one.

Cooper was frequently motivated by contrariety, and it is altogether possible that *Precaution* was so inspired. Certainly his next three novels seem to have been answers to challenges. When critics objected to *Precaution* on grounds that it was just another echo of English fiction, not the long awaited American novel, Cooper countered with two works of undeniably indigenous materials, *The*

Spy (1821), a tale of the Revolution, and *The Pioneers* (1823), at once a romance and a sociological novel about the frontier. Then he was taunted into writing *The Pilot* (1824), the first, and in some ways the most influential, of the eleven nautical tales he was to produce in his three decades of authorship.

At a dinner party in New York City Cooper listened with growing annoyance to the praise of Sir Walter Scott's latest romance, *The Pirate*. It was a book, the company generally agreed, that exhibited a high degree of nautical realism, all the more remarkable in that Sir Walter had enjoyed no firsthand acquaintance with seafaring. But Cooper *had* had the experience which his companions of Thè Bread and Cheese club as well as Scott lacked, and he proceeded to disabuse his listeners of the nautical accuracy of *The Pirate*. Could he do better himself? Certainly! And his evidence, produced within a few months, was *The Pilot*.

After the failure of his first novel, Cooper scored notable successes with his next three. *The Spy* quickly went through three editions, was translated into several European languages, and was soon adapted for the stage. So great was the excitement over this thrilling American romance and its young author that an eager audience awaited his next effort, and when *The Pioneers* appeared, it was a runaway best seller, 3,000 copies going on the first day. And well that it was, for Cooper had reached his financial nadir. Liens on his property had forced him to sell land at ruinous prices, and in 1823 even his household furnishings were seized at the request of his creditors. It was only the sudden flow of money from his publishers that saved Cooper from bankruptcy.

✑ ஐ

By 1826 the family fortune had at last been sufficiently repaired so that Cooper could take the European trip he had hopefully been planning for three or four years. It was to be in part an overdue vacation during which the novelist's failing health might be restored; it was to have educational value, offering the whole family the traditional Grand Tour of the Continent; and it was, hopefully, to bring financial profit as well: Cooper wished to make arrangements with European publishers in order to stave off pirate printers and to make the authorized European editions of his works more profitable. International copyright was more than half a century away, and foreign works could be freely reprinted and sold without any payment to either the author or the original publisher. To thwart the pirate printers, Cooper arranged with reliable publishers in several countries to bring out simultaneously the authorized edition of each future novel. This gave a definite sales advantage to the authorized publisher, for he alone could announce the forthcoming work and take orders in advance; and with a month needed by even the most efficient pirate to bring out a competing edition, he could skim the cream off the market. Unlike Dickens, who earned only dyspepsia and enmity from his petulant campaigning for copyright protection, Cooper quietly outwitted the harpies of the trade.

Friends and admirers in New York City organized a rousing send-off for Fenimore Cooper on the eve of his departure for Europe. (He had had "Fenimore" added to his name that year by an act of the Legislature, in order to perpetuate his mother's family name, threatened with extinction.) Members of his favorite group, a supper club of talented men who called their society The Bread and Cheese, sponsored an impressive testimonial dinner to which a host of notables were invited. Among them were DeWitt Clinton, Governor of New York; General Winfield Scott, hero of the War of 1812; Charles King, newspaper editor in the city and future president of Columbia University; and James Kent, former Chief Judge and Chancellor of the State of New York. In one toast King ranked Cooper with Sir Walter Scott, the "Great Enchanter of the North," and in another, Kent referred to him as "The genius which has rendered our native soil classic ground, and given to our early history the enchantments of fiction." Cooper was the country's first significant novelist, they realized, the man who had at last put America into fiction, and on his departure for Europe, no compliment was too fulsome, no praise too high. It is ironic that by the time of his return he had fallen from public grace, heckled widely by newspaper critics and suspected by a great many of his own countrymen. But that reversal of fortune was seven years away, and in the meantime Cooper was to enjoy a protracted holiday abroad.

After a month-long voyage to England, the Coopers proceeded to France where they spent nearly a year and a half in and around Paris. Awed tourists at first, the large Cooper family—there were six children including a nephew—spent its days sight-seeing and its evenings in retirement. But as the novelist's health improved and his presence in Paris was discovered by the international set, they moved into the social whirl of the world's most sociable city. General Lafayette, Princess Galitzin, and Mrs. James Brown, wife of the American Minister to France, all took it upon themselves to sponsor the strangers from America, and the salons of all Paris were opened to them. At the dinners and balls to which they were invited they were properly impressed by the glittering array of aristocratic and diplomatic titles, and in their letters home they frequently indulged in wholesale name dropping. Among the notable people Cooper met in Paris was another much-lionized foreign writer—with whom Cooper already had been compared—Sir Walter Scott, who was working at the time on a biography of Napoleon.

It was not until 1828 that the family left Paris to begin its tour proper, a journey to be reported in colorful detail in Cooper's five books of European travels. Returning to England, they then proceeded through the Low Countries to Switzerland, where they spent the summer in a rented villa on the outskirts of Berne. Cooper was enamoured of the Alpine scenery, and for the entire summer his writing gave way to excursions. His eldest daughter later wrote that he was "in a state of perpetual *toosy-moosy*," a term she used to indicate "an indescribable amount of poetical enjoyment." After viewing the routine tourist sights with his family, Cooper made several lengthy jaunts into the more remote and rugged sections of Switzerland, often traveling on foot, alone except for his guide. On one such rigorous hike of twelve days' duration, he walked over three hundred miles. But they had to leave before Cooper had explored all the cantons, and it was four years before another season in the Alps, this time on the shores of Lake Geneva, finally satisfied his curiosity about the tiny republic.

When autumn chilled the Alps in 1828, the Coopers went south through the Simplon Pass to Italy. At Florence they rented a ten-room apartment and lost themselves for nine months in a culture-fest, visiting art galleries, museums, and historic spots in the environs of this Queen City of the Italian Renaissance. In August they sailed by felucca from Leghorn to Naples and spent another nine months in leisurely progress back up the peninsula. Pompeii, Capri, Vesuvius, Rome, Venice, all the historic and scenic "musts" were on their itinerary. But Italy became more than just a sequence of tourist sights for Cooper; his letters and journals of this period indicate clearly that this was the one European country where what he met most became a part of him.

❧ ❧

After a brief trip to Dresden, Germany, they returned to Paris, which served as a headquarters for their last three years abroad. They arrived in the French capital on the heels of the 1830 July Revolution that deposed the last of the Bourbons, Charles X, and put Louis Philippe, the so-called Citizen King, on the throne. Cooper's old friend Lafayette, leader of the Republican party, had mistaken Philippe's expedient show of liberalism for idealism and had secured popular support for him when Charles fled; but as time went on, the new government came under the control of the wealthy bourgeoisie, who quickly edged Lafayette and his Republicans from the coalition. Cooper saw at first hand the intricate maneuvers of power politics during those first three years of the 1830's, and he tried to warn the too-trusting old General, in their conversations together, about the duplicity of his colleagues. He saw clearly that once again a small clique, grasping and ruthless, had captured power, this time behind the semblance of democratic principles; as Cooper discovered, to his chagrin, they were better able to hide their real motives under the banner of republicanism than under that of monarchy. This disconcerting truth was the theme of *The Bravo*, the first of the three politico-social novels about Europe that he undertook at this time and published between 1831 and 1833.

Cooper admired and respected Lafayette both for his role in the American Revolution and for his unselfish devotion to the cause of republican principles in France. The grand old soldier, who had been a living legend in America now for over half a century, was to him the model of democratic statesmanship, and Cooper felt honored by the invitations the General frequently extended to him and the family to visit at his suburban estate, La Grange. It is most ironic that almost all of the literary projects inspired by their friendship should redound to Cooper's discredit. The unlucky star that shone on Lafayette's declining years seems to have cast its baleful influence on all who came within his orbit.

Just after Cooper had arrived in Europe, Lafayette had requested him to write a book that would, in part at least, commemorate the General's triumphal tour of America in 1824–25.

COOPER'S CHILDREN, CRAYON DRAWING BY HIS DAUGHTER SUSAN ABOUT 1833
Caroline   Susan   Paul   Charlotte   Fanny

Realizing that a book-length sequence of receptions, welcoming speeches, testimonial dinners, and interviews would be deadly, Cooper hit upon an alternative acceptable to Lafayette: a book about America, correcting many of the European misunderstandings about the country, in which his friend would be a secondary character. In *Notions of the Americans, Picked up by a Travelling Bachelor* the narrator visits America, arriving at the same time as Lafayette and crossing his path at several points, and discovers that most of the published accounts of British travelers have badly misrepresented the United States, its manners, its morals, its politics, its religious revivalism, everything. In overcompensating for such inaccuracies Cooper wrote an impossible eulogy of the country that did not please British critics. Britons still patronized America—were not *they* the arbiters of taste?—and they resented the reprimand implicit in *Notions.* They attacked the book in such outraged tones that several Anglophilic American reviewers along the East Coast were automatically prejudiced against it. There were few who had a kind word for it. Without being drawn into the single-cause fallacy, one is forced to give some credence to Cooper's later contention that it was the bad reception of this book that started his decline from the heights of public favor.

A second literary effort to please Lafayette also boomeranged, and here the irony deepens. Lafayette decided to make the national budget a political issue in the Chamber of Deputies; he wished to embarrass his opponents of the Monarchist party with evidence that a republic was the least expensive form of government to administer. The enemy fired the first volley in the *Révue Britannique,* an attack on the high cost of operating various offices of the United States government, and Lafayette appealed to Cooper for a rebuttal. Guided partly by sentimental motives and partly by patriotic zeal, Cooper gathered materials on American finance and published the results in *Letter of J. Fenimore Cooper to General Lafayette* (1831), a document which Lafayette presented to the Chamber for its consideration. A heated debate ensued, and when several of the contestants moved from rostrum to press, Cooper found himself catapulted into a full-scale pamphlet war filled with charges and countercharges. It was practically a draw, the public and the great liberal newspaper *Le National* supporting Cooper and Lafayette, despite heavy opposition from the numerous political papers of the powerful Conservative groups. At the critical moment, however, the new American minister, William Rives, playing politics for his own diplomatic purposes, sided with the ruling Monarchist party and tipped the balance in their favor. A later Congressional investigation was to show clearly that Cooper's statistics on government finance were more accurate than those supplied by the American minister, but by then the cause had been lost.

◄§ §►

The support that Cooper had expected from the American press during the Finance Controversy failed to materialize; instead, he was criticized at home for becoming involved in such an affair. Who was he to offend a foreign government? Cooper had often been annoyed at Americans who curried favor with Europeans by deprecating the various institutions of their own country, and his fury now at what he saw as toadying by Rives and a number of American journalists was no secret. It was at this point in his worsening public relations that Cooper committed the error in judgment that, as things progressed, earned him the enmity of the American press for the remainder of his life. The *New York American* reversed its favorable evaluation of *The Bravo,* and inasmuch as its second review was apparently based on the French edition of the novel, Cooper, unduly influenced by the suspicions of his slightly paranoid friend Samuel F. B. Morse, rather too hastily concluded that there was collusion between the paper and agents of the Monarchist party. Such was not the case. Cooper then proceeded to compound his error with indiscretion by accusing the *American* of foul play. The result was disastrous, for in the heated exchange that followed he alienated a sizable segment of the press, and so great did the hostility of many editors become that Cooper-baiting became a sport among them. When he finally returned to the United States in 1833, he was no longer the darling of the American people he had been at his departure seven years before. His friends of The Bread and Cheese rallied round him and offered to stage a grand homecoming dinner, but he graciously declined their gesture of loyalty and quietly withdrew from the society of New York City to the seclusion of Cooperstown. Despite further unpopularity at home, before his death in 1851 Cooper was to be recognized as America's first master of the novel.

2

✑ THE QUEST FOR
AN AMERICAN NOVEL

For some time the novel as a literary form did not fare well in the English-speaking New World. It was two hundred years after the arrival of the *Mayflower* when Cooper, who was to become America's first recognized novelist, started his career with the publication of *Precaution*. There had, of course, been earlier attempts. *The Power of Sympathy* (1789), by William Hill Brown, is now generally credited with being the first American novel. It was the beginning of a long run of novels of seduction, sentimental works in the manner of Richardson, father of the type in England. Among these American imitations are Susanna Rowson's *Charlotte Temple* (1794) and Hannah Foster's *The Coquette* (1797), of interest today more as period pieces than as works of art.

Of greatest fame among Cooper's predecessors in America was Charles Brockden Brown, the author of Gothic tales of terror. An impassioned, undisciplined writer with ambitions that overreached his limited artistic ability, Brown did, however ineffectually, use American settings for his works, and in one of them, *Edgar Huntly,* is the best pre-Cooperian chapter on the Indian.

Only one other writer before Cooper's time stands out among the hundred or so who tried and failed to write a great American novel: Hugh Henry Brackenridge. A political satirist who explored both the strengths and the weaknesses of American democracy, he was also the first American to employ in his writing the picaresque techniques made popular by Cervantes and continued by his eighteenth-century imitators, notably Fielding and Smollett. Brackenridge labored long over a multivolume work which he finally titled *Modern Chivalry* and brought out in six parts between 1792 and 1815, when he republished the whole in a complete, uniform four-volume edition. Its two central characters, Captain Farrago, bachelor, philosopher, spectator of life, and Teague O'Regan, his illiterate Irish servant, bear some resemblances to Don Quixote and Sancho Panza. Aside from the slapstick humor involved in Teague's numerous escapades, the book held relatively little appeal for a popular audience; it was too erudite, at times even pedantic, and, actually only superficially American, was never acknowledged as a work of art that spoke for its time and place.

≈§ §≈

With these the high points of novelistic achievement nearly half a century after the Declaration of Independence, Sydney Smith, one of the founders of the *Edinburgh Review,* was not entirely unjustified in his cutting question, "Who reads an American book?" One can understand the increasingly impatient cry from editors and critics for an acceptable native American novel. Washington Irving had been appropriately hailed, both at home and in Europe, as America's first man of letters, but he had disappointed many by limiting himself in the area of prose fiction to the short tale. It was the full-length work, the story with epic proportions, that was eagerly awaited; and with Cooper's second novel, *The Spy,* most of the reviewers thought that this goal had finally been at least approached. Even the Olympian *North American Review* found it to be "fiction of the highest order of romantic interest," and admitted, after the appropriate reservations of a Yankee journal toward a New Yorker, that Cooper was "the first who has deserved the appellation of a distinguished American novel writer." The reviewer, W. H. Gardiner, also saw clearly the greater contribution Cooper made in leading the way to an American literature. He had, declared Gardiner, "laid the foundations of American romance."

In referring to Cooper as a writer of the "romance," the reviewers were automatically associating him with Great Britain's most eminent prose writer of the day, Sir Walter Scott. The term "romance" had been applied to the historical novels by Scott to indicate their removal from the day-to-day realism of a *Robinson Crusoe* or a social novel by his contemporary, Jane Austen. In his historical novels, beginning with *Waverly* in 1814, Scott had used melodrama and spectacle to heighten the action, picturesque setting and pageantry to add color to the scene, and either high sensibility or rustic quaintness (depending on the social level) to distinguish his characters. He had also managed to cast an air of mystery over his tales that removed them still further from ordinary life. All these devices Cooper too employed in varying degrees—while the American poet Whittier was imitating another Scotsman, Robert Burns—and it was not long before Cooper was being called "the American Scott." The epithet often implied equality with "The Wizard of the North" as well as indebtedness to him, though there is no question about the latter. Without Scott's example and the seemingly ubiquitous market for romances which Scott almost singlehandedly had created, Cooper could not have achieved so great a success as a writer in such a remarkably short space of time, the five years between 1821 and 1826.

About the indigenous qualities of *The Spy*, however, there could be little doubt: its setting was Westchester County, New York; its action was related to a recognizable part of the Revolutionary War; among its identifiable historical characters was George Washington, alias Mr. Harper; and among its type characters were such folk figures as a Yankee peddler and an Uncle Tom variety of the Negro slave.

During part of the Revolutionary War, Westchester County was the no-man's land between the Continental forces to the north along the Hudson River and the British forces, who held New York City, to the south. As the subtitle of the novel indicates, the area was known at the time as "The Neutral Ground," but it was a restless place aboil with guerrilla forays of Cowboys (British) and Skinners (Patriots) and espionage activities. In Cooper's story, threading his way deftly through its maze of duplicity is Washington's key spy, the pack-peddler Harvey Birch. With a pass from Sir Henry Clinton, who thinks him a Loyalist, Harvey acts as agent of both the Patriot espionage and counterespionage systems; in the process he is hunted and harried by both sides, though, ironically, more severely by the Americans whom he serves. His life is a continuous cycle of pursuit-capture-escape-and pursuit, a progression of action that was to animate many of Cooper's future works. So involved does Harvey become with the secrets of both camps that Washington orders him never to reveal his true role, and herein lies his tragedy, for he must live out the rest of his life suspected by many of his friends of having been a supporter of the Crown. This was the penalty he foresaw, however, when he undertook his difficult and dangerous mission, and he is faithful to his pledge of silence. All in all, Harvey's self-sacrificing but humble patriotism; the shadowy presence of the demigod Washington; a family split in its allegiance to king and country, as many were divided during the Revolution; and a conventional comedy of young lovers combine to make *The Spy* a highly readable book.

Issued and reissued in a flow of new editions, adapted for the stage, and translated into several European languages, *The Spy* was a publishing success that launched the careers both of James Fenimore Cooper and of the American novel. Whether or not they would prosper was another question. There were odds against the development of an American literature; Cooper voiced them clearly in 1828 in *Notions of the Americans,* and over three decades later Nathaniel Hawthorne was still repeating the second of them in his preface to *The Marble Faun.* The first major obstacle that Cooper saw was an economic one:

> The fact that an American publisher can get an English work without money must for a few years longer . . . have a tendency to repress a national literature. No man will pay a writer for an epic, a tragedy, a sonnet, a history, or a romance when he can get a work of equal merit for nothing.
>
> A capital American publisher has assured me that there are not a dozen writers in this country whose works he should feel confidence in publishing at all, while he reprints hundreds of English books without the least hesitation. This preference is by no means so much owing to any difference in merit, as to the fact that, when the price of the original author is to be added to the uniform hazard which accompanies all literary speculation, the risk becomes too great.

Should this difficulty somehow be overcome, there was still what seemed to many the more basic problem of inadequate artistic resources. Could a raw frontier republic actually support a literature? Cooper's "Travelling Bachelor" remarks:

> "There is scarcely an ore which contributes to the wealth of the author that is found here in veins as rich as in Europe. There are no annals for the historian; no follies (beyond the most vulgar and commonplace) for the satirist; no manners for the dramatist; no obscure fictions for the writer of romance; no gross and hardy offences against decorum for the moralist. . . . The weakest hand can extract a spark from the flint, but it would baffle the strength of a giant to attempt kindling a flame with a pudding-stone."

Hawthorne's words, written in England in 1859, echo these thoughts:

> No author, without a trial, can conceive of the difficulty of writing a romance about a country where there is no shadow, no antiquity, no mystery, no picturesque and gloomy wrong, nor anything but a commonplace prosperity, in broad and simple daylight, as is happily the case with my dear native land. . . . Romance and poetry, ivy, lichens, and wallflowers, need ruin to make them grow.

Cooper led the way in removing both obstacles. Sales of his books were sufficient to keep major publishers bidding for new manuscripts from his pen—in America, Carey of Philadelphia (after the death of Cooper's first publisher, Wiley), and in England the house of Bentley. The Carey firm published only two American novels prior to 1820; between 1820 and 1830 it brought out thirty-four; and in the next decade it added another one hundred and forty-two. In self-defense, other publishing houses were forced to increase their search for native talent. The Carey records show clearly the integral part Cooper played in this newly discovered salability of American fiction. As to the poverty of materials in the New World, his own productivity belied the validity of that argument. In the thirty years between *Precaution* (1820) and *The Ways of the Hour* (1850), he published thirty-two novels, the same number as Scott's total output, as well as more than a dozen other works.

Cooper used in his fiction several different patterns, for he did not continue to be exclusively a writer of historical novels after the success of *The Spy*. Even before he suffered a major setback in 1825 with the failure of *Lionel Lincoln,* a historical novel about Lexington, Concord, and Bunker Hill, he had demonstrated his ability to write the romance of the forest, beginning in 1823 with *The Pioneers,* and the romance of the sea, with *The Pilot* the following year. In abandoning his projected series "Legends of the Thirteen Republics" after *Lionel Lincoln* revealed his limitations as a writer of historical fiction, he freed himself to develop those species of the genre most suited to his background and talent.

That the romance of the forest was his forte Cooper proved with his most popular series, the *Leather-Stocking Tales,* and three other individual volumes. The American wilderness had long stirred romantic imaginations, both at home and abroad. Even Byron, otherwise almost oblivious of the New World, had been moved to linger in his *Don Juan* over a eulogy on the well-known frontier figure, Daniel Boone. It was the excited but still shapeless flow of feelings about the wilderness and its inhabitants, red and white, that Cooper crystallized in his forest romances. The *Leather-Stocking Tales,* filled with bloodcurdling Indian warfare and the breathtaking adventures of the remarkable scout Natty Bumppo, cast a long shadow, in history still influencing the image of the frontier, and in literature providing the prototype for to-day's "western."

For his romances of the sea Cooper's chief indebtedness was to the eighteenth-century Scottish novelist, Tobias Smollett. In two of his novels, *Roderick Random* and *Peregrine Pickle,* Smollett had developed memorable caricatures of seamen, and a few pages of each of these novels were set at sea. But the sea was only the pathway *to* adventure with Smollett, not the pathway *of* adventure. *The Pilot* and Cooper's ten other nautical tales are all pursuit-and-escape stories that take place on the high seas instead of in the ports along the way. So greatly did he shape the nautical novel that Carl Van Doren, historian of American fiction, credits Cooper with being the father of the genre.

Romance gave way to realism as the problems of Cooper's personal life began to mount. In his later years he turned more often to fiction as the vehicle for his criticism of the times. Seven of his novels fall into this category, some of his poorest works and a couple that come close to his best. Where the narrative predominates and he remains the storyteller, as in *Satanstoe*, Cooper is at his most winning; he becomes proportionately less and less effective as an artist as his ratio of "message" increases, until a novel such as *The Redskins* seems more a tract than a tale.

At the risk of being somewhat arbitrary in the classification, one can separate Cooper's novels into five types:

I. Society Novel
    Precaution (1820)
II. Historical Novels
    The Spy (1821)
    Lionel Lincoln (1825)
III. Romances of the Forest
    The Pioneers (1823)
    The Last of the Mohicans (1826)
    The Prairie (1827)
    The Wept of Wish-ton-Wish (1829)
    The Pathfinder (1840)
    The Deerslayer (1841)
    Wyandotté (1843)
    The Oak Openings (1848)
IV. Nautical Novels
    The Pilot (1824)
    The Red Rover (1828)
    The Water-Witch (1831)
    Homeward Bound (1838)
    * *Mercedes of Castile* (1840)
    The Two Admirals (1842)
    The Wing-and-Wing (1842)
    Afloat and Ashore (1842)
    Miles Wallingford (1842)
    Jack Tier (1848)
    The Sea Lions (1849)
V. Socio-political Novels
    * *The Bravo* (1831)
    * *The Heidenmauer* (1832)
    * *The Headsman* (1833)
    The Monikins (1835)
    Home as Found (1838)
    Satanstoe (1845)
    The Chainbearer (1845)

The Redskins (1846)
The Crater (1847)
The Ways of the Hour (1850)
(Starred items could also be listed under II.)

In almost all of these works Cooper drew heavily from folk sources for his material. Although he clearly gained much from the literary tradition, he derived even more from the oral. Many of his characters are folk types, some of them stock figures from English literature but others distinctly American. No writer before Cooper had delineated so clearly the features of the frontiersman, the retreating red man, the Yankee, the squatter, or the American Negro. Their manners, their habits, and their customs can be seen in his pages, their beliefs and superstitions can be felt, and what is more significant, their *voices* can be heard. Cooper had an ear remarkably well attuned to folk speech, and he went much farther than any writer to his time toward capturing dialect. Over a thousand proverbs and folk sayings are uttered by his characters, and a number of different speech patterns give them geographical and professional distinctness. His Yankees, for example, exhibit a number of the linguistic peculiarities that later scholars have identified as unmistakable New Englandisms; his seamen use a salty lingo filled with hundreds of nautical terms current in the days of the clipper ships; and Natty Bumppo speaks a dialect of his own, which for all its ungrammatical and somewhat archaic constructions is peculiarly rhythmical and poetic. No other writer in his own time and few since have used folklore as extensively or as effectively as Cooper did.

❧ ❧

Cooper's eminence as the first important American novelist was widely acknowledged abroad long before his death, and translations of his works were available in all of the languages of Western Europe as well as in such less familiar tongues as Persian, Egyptian, and Turkic. His friend Samuel F. B. Morse reported after a tour abroad that Cooper's novels "are published as soon as he produces them in thirty-four different places in Europe." Everywhere they were read eagerly by young and old. As the composer Franz Schubert lay dying in Vienna in 1828, he requested a friend to rush to him the latest Cooper book in print, having

27

read two of the three *Leather-Stocking Tales* then published, as well as *The Spy* and *The Pilot*.

Certainly some of Cooper's vogue abroad can be attributed to his early recognition by leading writers of Europe. Balzac, Dumas, George Sand, Scott, Thackeray, Goethe, and the Russian critic Belinsky all extolled his novels. A typical example of their enthusiastic response to his work can be seen in Balzac's review of *The Pathfinder* in the *Révue Parisienne* of July 25, 1840:

> Here Cooper becomes again the great Cooper. The description of the forests, the waters of the river and its rapids, the tricks of the savages which the Big Serpent, Jasper, and the Pathfinder foil, make a series of marvellous pictures. Such passages are the despair of every novelist who has tried to follow in the footsteps of the American author. Never has topographical writing encroached further upon painting. This is the school where the literary landscape painter should study; all the secrets of the art are here. From page to page the dangers present themselves naturally; there is no attempt to set the stage. You yourself seem to bend down, under the great trees, to note the print of a moccasin. . . . It is impossible to separate the earth, the trees, the waters from the incidents of the story which excite you. And the characters become . . . of small account against the great scene you scan without ceasing.

Cooper's reception in France, Germany, Spain, and Italy has been the subject of numerous studies by scholars. They have shown that he exerted an appreciable influence on the literature of those countries, especially on that of France. In Balzac's fierce peasants of *Les Chouans* (1829) one finds a Gallic version of Cooper's Indians, and his red men are also the models for Dumas' underworld characters in the admittedly imitative novel *Les Mohicans de Paris* (1854). A number of lesser luminaries such as Eugène Sue, Gabriel Ferry, and Gustave Aimard became devoted disciples, turning out dozens of volumes of Cooperesque fiction, adapting to their own purposes both his romances of the forest and his tales of the sea. Pierre Jean David, the noted French sculptor, carved a classic bust of Cooper, and when it was completed he wrote to the novelist that he was going to have copies made to send to admirers of the American in several French cities. When Cooper died, another French artist, the romantic composer Berlioz, paid tribute to him by renaming one of his overtures *Le corsaire rouge* after Cooper's best-liked sea novel among French readers, *The Red Rover*.

◅§ §▻

Sydney Smith's question had been answered: Almost everyone, it seems, was reading an American book by the time of Cooper's death in 1851. In 1850 Hawthorne had published *The Scarlet Letter*, and in 1851 Melville, one of Cooper's admirers, brought forth *Moby Dick*. Just thirty years after its birth with *The Spy*, the American novel had come of age.

3

THE TRAGIC WILDERNESS

Of Cooper's thirty-two novels, eight are set on the ever westering frontier that his own family had known as it passed through central New York. The *Leather-Stocking Tales* account for only five of these novels about pioneer life, and yet in popularity they have outweighed all of Cooper's other works combined. Even as he worked on them he sensed that these romances of the American wilderness were to be his chief claim to immortality:

> If anything from the pen of the writer of these romances is at all to outlive himself, it is, unquestionably, the series of the "Leather-Stocking Tales." To say this, is not to predict a very lasting reputation for the series itself, but simply to express the belief it will outlast any, or all, of the works from the same hand.

The *Tales* form a five-volume biography of their protagonist Natty Bumppo, from his young manhood among the Delaware Indians in New York and Pennsylvania to his death, in his early eighties, among the Pawnee tribes just west of the Mississippi River. On the level of plot they are a series of thrilling episodes filled with Indian warfare and the struggle of rival empires for control of a continent. But the *Tales* are obviously more than melodrama. They are a saga of the roughhewing of America. By his imaginative treatment of the conquering of the wilderness—his re-creation of the generations of men and women who established civilization, or were destroyed by it, in the New World—Cooper was serving as mythmaker. There is little doubt now that much of his appeal in the nineteenth century derived from this mythopoeic faculty. His romantic image of the frontier, with its steadily advancing white settlers and its forever retreating red men, shaped the thinking of readers both at home and abroad—not only directly, through the novels themselves, but indirectly as well through the writings of those historians, among whom Francis Parkman was perhaps the most influential, who came under Cooper's spell. So inextricably was the Leather-Stocking myth woven into the American design that when Pershing's troops landed in France in 1917, one of the French leaders purportedly observed, "The spirit of Leather-Stocking is awake."

◆§ §◆

Just ahead of the settlers in the eighteenth and nineteenth centuries moved another breed of men almost as exotic as the Indians with whom they associated. These were the Boones, the Cocketts, the Carsons, advance scouts thrown out by civilization for one of the longest overland marches in its history. Driven by a variety of motives—discontent, misanthropy, restiveness, adventurousness—these individuals separated from the main body of society to live alone in the still uncharted reaches of the forest. But the knowledge and skills they acquired there put their services in high demand, and ironically, they were often called upon to be the agents for a way of life they had tried to flee. They blazed trails, hunted game, located potable water, negotiated with the Indians, and, in general, taught the pioneer families how to survive in the great American wilderness. Then when the crush of humanity and the restrictions of society became unbearable in the new settlements they had helped to establish, they pushed still farther westward, only to be overtaken again and again till the land gave way to the sea and the cycle was finally halted. As if by some master plan, they stepped forth at the moment they were needed, fulfilled their purpose, and then were consumed by the creature they served. As Parkman observed:

Civilization has a destroying as well as a creating power. It is exterminating the buffalo and the Indian. . . . It must, moreover, eventually sweep from before it a class of men, its own precursors . . . so remarkable both in their virtues and their faults that few men will see their extinction without regret.

This man whom civilization itself destroyed is, in the twentieth century, still remembered. William Faulkner, in *Requiem for a Nun,* describes a very unidealized frontiersman, whose own dispossession Faulkner, like Parkman, recognizes:

. . . then came the Anglo-Saxon, the pioneer, the tall man . . . turning the earth into a howling waste from which he would be the first to vanish, not even on the heels but synchronous with the slightly darker wild men whom he had dispossessed, because, like them, only the wilderness could feed and nourish him; and so disappeared . . . leaving his ghost . . . haunting the fringes of the wilderness which he himself had helped to destroy. . . .

Of this class of men whose loss has thus been noted in two centuries, James Fenimore Cooper's Leather-Stocking is the *beau ideal.* He is at once a sharply individualized representative of the type, and beyond that a mythical hero who symbolizes the whole phase of history in which the type flourished.

Natty Bumppo's origin, like that of many another mythical hero, is shrouded in mystery. Vaguely he remembers the white home of his very early childhood, and occasionally he alludes to it in a cryptic manner, but precisely where it was and what caused him to depart from it are questions that Cooper does not answer. All that is told about the years before the opening of *The Deerslayer,* in which he appears as a young man, is that he was reared by Moravian missionaries among the friendly Delawares. The instruction of the Brethren seems to have been limited to the Gospel, for Natty remains illiterate and largely uninformed about the world without the wilderness. Formally adopted by the Delawares as he approaches manhood, he casts his earthly lot unmistakably with that of the red man, and yet, significantly, he never becomes so thoroughly Indianized that he turns his hand against his own people or forsakes basic Christian ethics. "A magnificent moral hermaphrodite," Balzac called him, "between the savage and civilized states."

32

THE LEATHER–STOCKING TALES

Title	Name Given Natty Bumppo	Age of Natty Bumppo	Date of Action	Setting	Year Published
The Deerslayer	Deerslayer	Early 20's	1740's	Otsego Lake	1841
The Last of the Mohicans	Hawkeye	Mid-30's	1757	Glens Falls, Lake George	1826
The Pathfinder	Pathfinder	Late 30's	1759	Lake Ontario	1840
The Pioneers	Leather-Stocking	Early 70's	1793	Cooperstown	1823
The Prairie	the trapper, the old man	80's	1804	Iowa, Missouri	1827

The Leather-Stocking stories illustrate Natty's identification with the Indian throughout various stages of the settling of America, as well as the Indian's shifting role on the American frontier. In *The Deerslayer* Natty confirms his oath of allegiance to a young Delaware chief, Chingachgook, by risking his life in a seemingly hopeless battle to rescue his friend's beloved, Wah-ta-Wah. Their continuing companionship, which is to be lifelong, is portrayed in four of the books and recalled by Natty in the fifth. He allies with the red men in other ways too. In *The Pathfinder* his ultimate temptation to join civilization is overcome when he renounces all claim to the hand of Mabel Dunham. By the time of *The Pioneers* he has lived so long under the laws of nature that he is not only uncomfortable in the town of Templeton, where duty holds him temporarily, but he is completely bewildered by the man-made laws encountered there. The book is an object lesson in the painful progress from noble savagery to noble civilization, a cultural journey which Natty is neither willing nor able to complete; instead, he travels west to spend his last days on the Great Plains among the Pawnees, in what Richard Chase has called the Götterdämmerung of the Leather-Stocking series, *The Prairie*. Yet each of the *Tales* also emphasizes the fact that Natty, despite his Indian habits, is fundamentally a white man. The reader is continually reminded of it, from the opening pages of *The Deerslayer* through all five volumes to the last day of Natty's life, when he requests that the gravestone promised him be inscribed with "something from the holy book."

James Fenimore Cooper

The figure that evolves is a white man committed to white ethics but rejecting white society; a white man, furthermore, devoid of all the traditional prejudices, pro and con, about Indians, and hence left free to form his own opinions about them. From the unique vantage point at which circumstances have placed him, Natty is able to view both aboriginal and civilized groups with an unprecedented detachment that brings him to espouse a crude theory of cultural relativity which evaluates all human action in terms of its social context. Conceding that men are "in the main, much the same in feelin's," Natty ascribes their differences to cultural traits which he calls *gifts*. He thus explains his theory in *The Deerslayer:*

> "God made us all, white, black, and red; and no doubt, had his wise intentions in coloring us differently. . . . I'll not deny that he gave each race its gifts. A white man's gifts are Christianized, while a redskin's are more for the wilderness. Thus it would be a great offense for a white man to scalp the dead; whereas it's a signal vartue for an Indian. Then ag'in, a white man cannot amboosh women and children in war, while a redskin may. 'Tis *cruel* work, I'll allow; but for them it's *lawful* work; while for *us*, it would be grievous work."

Later in the same book Natty reasons that "gifts come of circumstances. . . . and excuse a thousand acts and idees."

He does not speculate on the possibility that the underlying human kinship might in the end prevail over the traits induced by training. Eventual assimilation of the Indian is not even suggested, for the mingling of red and white would mean interracial marriage, and the taboo against this step was one which Cooper did not care to, or dare to, break. There may be one Lord of all, and in the mind of God all men may be the same, so that in heaven Chingachgook's son Uncas may be united with his Cora Munro, but on earth there must be no such interaction between the two peoples. The inviolability of this taboo made both the Leather-Stocking story and the frontier saga it idealized inescapably tragic. Settlers surging irrepressibly westward were lopping off mile after mile of the vast areas necessary to maintain a hunting culture, and even as early as the 1820's the fate of the red man was plainly written for all to see: unable to "lick" the land-hungry whites and unwelcome to join them, the Indian was

34

doomed to extinction. Taught by the Moravians to identify all human fortune with the will of a benevolent deity, Natty Bumppo is too devout to strike out, Promethean fashion, at these palpably gross injustices, but his grudging and sorrowful acceptance of its inevitability invests the whole Leather-Stocking series with an aura of melancholy. Partly within and partly above this tragic saga, the frontiersman serves in the triple function of prophet, victim, and instrument of atonement.

Natty's concern for the Indian develops in two stages; it is at first limited to the plight of his own adoptive tribe, the Delawares, in relation solely to savage society, but it later evolves into a lament for the whole Indian race confronted by the white man. With their greatness destroyed by the Iroquois, the Delaware-Mohicans, "scattered as the sands of the dry river-beds fly before the fall hurricanes," are a fallen people comforted only by nostalgic memories of better days. An elegiac note is struck by Natty at the very beginning of the *Leather-Stocking Tales* when, by way of exposition, he briefs Harry March on the character of Chingachgook:

> "If he had his rights, he would be a great chief; but, as it is, he is only a brave and just-minded Delaware; respected, and even obeyed in some things, 'tis true, but of a fallen race and belonging to a fallen people. Ah! Harry March, 'twould warm the heart within you to sit in their lodges of a winter's night, and listen to the traditions of the ancient greatness and power of the Mohicans!"

With the decline of Delaware influence, the noblest elements of savage life have succumbed to the meanest, and the dominance of the "accursed Mingoes," as Natty calls the fierce Iroquois, bodes but evil for the rest of the Indian world. This is the source of that occasional touch of sadness which beclouds the otherwise innocent happiness of *The Deerslayer*.

Melancholy reflection on the decline of the Delawares recurs time and again throughout the *Tales,* at its peak, perhaps, during the funeral rites for Uncas at the end of *The Last of the Mohicans,* the second volume in the legend. But in the closing lines of that book the venerable Tammany, advising his people that "The pale-faces are the masters of the earth, and the time of the red-men has not yet come again," foresees that the fall of the Delawares is emblematic of the fate of all Indians. From then on, the Delawares' plight becomes a subsidiary theme as Natty, looking beyond the internal affairs of the Indians to the forces that threaten them from without, despairs for the whole race.

The bitter unfairness of the final situation is conveyed by an unrecognizably old and broken Chingachgook in the fourth component of the chronicle, *The Pioneers:*

> "Did they [the white men] say to him [the Indian], Brother, sell us your land, and take this gold, this silver, these blankets, these rifles, or even this rum? No; they tore it from him, as a scalp is torn from an enemy; and they that did it looked not behind them, to see whether he lived or died."

Natty's sorrow for this truth is expressed later in the same work when even old Chingachgook is dead:

> "When I look about me, at these hills, where I used to could count sometimes twenty smokes, curling over the tree-tops, from the Delaware camps, it raises mournful thoughts, to think that not a red-skin is left of them all. . . ."

But of the many characters who filled the pages of fiction, drama, and poetry with lament for the red man, what distinguishes Natty is his personal involvement in the retreat. Unlike the armchair primitivists who theorized about the simple life and savage virtues, Natty tests empirically the values of a hunting culture, finds them attractive, and adopts many of them as his own. Throughout his life he clings to the ways of the hunter, relinquishing them only when the infirmity of advanced age reduces him to the related role of trapper. When his own people call upon him at critical moments for aid in their fight against the wilderness, his Christian conscience demands that he assist them, but in so doing he knows full well that he is killing the only thing he really loves—*loves* in a very literal sense. When Judith Hutter of *The Deerslayer,* Cooper's most charming hussy, asks the hunter where his sweetheart is, Natty replies earnestly:

> "She's in the forest, Judith—hanging from the boughs of the trees, in a soft rain—in the dew on the open grass—the clouds that float about in the blue heavens—the birds that sing in the woods—the sweet springs where I slake my thirst—and in all the other glorious gifts that come from God's Providence!"

It is this forest, the object of his love as well as the source of his subsistence, that the settlers of his own race must destroy in order to establish their particular way of life. In *The Pioneers* Natty accuses the heirs of Major Effingham of ruining the woodlands: "You have made the game so scarce and shy that better shots than him [Chingachgook] find it hard to get a livelihood"; he flees the town of Templeton, "where the hammer is sounding in my ears from sunrise to sundown," and yet, significantly, it was he himself who had helped the Major pioneer the area years before. Seeming, by such actions, to have discerned intuitively that the civilization in which he cannot participate is of a higher order than the savagism he enjoys, Natty becomes a co-operative victim of American progress westward, at times, as Roy Harvey Pearce has pointed out, "even a Christ-like figure, offering himself for a sacrifice."

How many readers who have, consciously or unconsciously, seen in the life of Natty Bumppo a messianic function is indeterminable, but it can be hazarded that at one time or another in their lives most thoughtful Americans have experienced feelings of guilt for the ruthless and criminal dispossession of the Indian. One catches occasional echoes of a national guilt in the works of important writers from Cooper and Melville to Maxwell Anderson in the North, from Cable to Faulkner in the South, from Miller to La Farge in the West; and during the nineteenth century it became a staple of the sentimental literature about the red man, a genre that reached a peak of popularity with Helen Hunt Jackson's *Ramona* in 1884.

Beset with this remorse, Americans only were provided a measure of atonement in the spectacle of the white man, in the person of the frontiersman, being offered up on the same altar of progress with the red man and the buffalo, in the sacrifice recognized by Parkman when he observed that civilization extirpates its own harbingers. And if the white men thus martyred afforded partial expiation for the annihilation of the Indians, in the Leather-Stocking myth Cooper delineated their redemptive destiny, providing a means for satisfying a psychic need felt keenly by nineteenth-century Americans and to a lesser degree by Europeans; in the figure of Natty Bumppo, Cooper gave America its first distinct messiah image.

Natty's rejection in *The Pathfinder* by a girl who prefers to marry a better-educated young man is only one indication of the wise but illiterate frontiersman's eventual dismissal by his own people. Years later in *The Pioneers*, when the community that has invaded his seclusion now molests the once essential old scout and finally sends a party to the woods to arrest him, the fate Natty deplores is comparable to that of the Indians:

> "What would ye with an old and helpless man? . . . You've driven God's creatures from the wilderness, where his providence had put them for his own pleasure; and you've brought in the troubles and diviltries of the law, where no man was ever known to disturb another. You have driven me, that have lived forty long years of my appointed time in this very spot, from my home and the shelter of my head, lest you should put your wicked feet and wasty ways in my cabin. You've driven me to burn these logs, under which I've eaten and drunk . . . for the half of a hundred years; and to mourn the ashes under my feet. . . . You've rankled the heart of an old man, that has never harmed you or your'n, with bitter feelings toward his kind . . . and now, when he has come to see the last brand of his hut, before it is melted into ashes, you follow him up, at midnight, like hungry hounds on the track of a worn-out and dying deer. What more would ye have? for I am here—one too many."

The force that finally pushes the scout out of his "beloved forests" to die a trapper on the plains, Cooper defines in his introduction to *The Prairie* as "desperate resignation." Natty cannot protest the realization that, along with the Indians, he has lost his place in and is being driven from his homeland, a forfeit to civilization.

Ironically, the literature which today carries on the tradition of Leather-Stocking has removed the hero completely from that very association with the Indians on which his cultural significance was founded. As Henry Nash Smith and David B. Davis have cogently demonstrated, the direct descendants of Natty, after spending a generation with the Indian fighters and "mountain men" and another with the Deadwood Dicks and the Buffalo Bills in the dime novel world of Erastus Beadle, evolved finally into the flamboyant ten-gallon hero of Western romance. These movie and television idols of the small fry (and their parents!) retain Natty's independence, his love of solitude, his homely knight-errantry, some traces of his dialect, and all of his aversion to a settled life, eschewing, as he did, both the entanglements of matrimony and the ownership of land. But except for an occasional Lone Ranger-Tonto relationship, they seem to have lost all contact with the red men. Like Natty, they flee conventional society for a less regularized way of life, but with the wilderness and its natives gone they have no state of savagism with which to identify. From a cultural point of view they are utter anachronisms, but, resplendent in their costumes and swashbuckling in their behavior, they live on grandly to perpetuate the Leather-Stocking myth in unending cycles of melodrama.

꿏 꿏

Beneath the symbolic value embodied in the figure of Natty Bumppo stands the man himself. What manner of man is he? This question is asked of the young gentleman Middleton in *The Prairie,* and his answer furnishes a brief but accurate appraisal of the hunter:

> "The man I speak of was of great simplicity of mind, but of sterling worth. Unlike most of those who live a border life, he united the better instead of the worst qualities of the two people [Indians and whites]. He was a man endowed with the choicest and perhaps rarest gift of nature; that of distinguishing good from evil. His virtues were those of simplicity, because such were the fruits of his habits, as were indeed his very prejudices. In courage he was the equal of his red associates; in warlike skill, being better instructed, their superior."

Simplicity and courage were qualities commonly attributed to the American borderers, but not moral discrimination. As Natty himself admits, the average was more often "a drunken, worthless vagabond," morally his inferior. It is this major difference which quickly converts from comparison to contrast any analogy between Cooper's hero and the stereotyped borderman.

Of the number of real-life frontiersmen who had come to the attention of the reading public before Leather-Stocking made his debut in 1823, none was of greater stature than Daniel Boone, and here there are grounds for comparison, for the influence of the Kentuckian on Cooper is evident. There are clear parallels between the lives of Bumppo and Boone, especially the Boone who emerged from magazine accounts of the 1810's and 1820's and was the subject of the frequently fictitious "autobiography" of 1823. This was Boone the Fugitive as opposed to Boone the Empire Builder. This was Boone the innocent, kindhearted, and carefree isolate whom Byron eulogized at some length in *Don Juan*. In the opening pages of *The Prairie* Cooper prepares for Natty's entrance by making a direct reference to "the patriarch of Kentucky":

> This adventurous and venerable patriarch was now seen making his last remove; placing the endless river between him and the multitude his own success had drawn around him, and seeking for the renewal of enjoyments which were rendered worthless in his eyes, when trammelled by the forms of human institutions.

Cooper's footnote to this passage leaves no doubt that it was the legendary rather than the historical Boone that appealed to him.

It seems likely that Cooper modeled Natty's attire and at least some of his physical features after other frontiersmen less illustrious but perhaps known personally to him during his youth in Otsego County. In a preface to a late edition of the *Leather-Stocking Tales* he wrote about his sources:

> The author has often been asked if he had any original in his mind for the character of Leather-Stocking. In a physical sense, different individuals known to the writer in early life certainly presented themselves as models, through his recollections. . . .

Claims have been made for a number of models, including various members of the Shipman family, neighbors of the author in Cooperstown. More likely candidates, in some respects, are several of the Indian fighters of New York State—Tom Quick, Tim Murphy, Nat Foster, Nick Stoner—whose exploits Harold W. Thompson has recounted in his best-selling volume of folklore, *Body, Boots & Britches*. But as Cooper himself said, Natty Bumppo was, in a moral sense, entirely imaginary, and except for certain physical traits he had no prototype.

What immediately strikes the reader of the *Leather-Stocking Tales* is the essential goodness of their hero. Rough, unsophisticated, and illiterate though he may be, Natty is easily recognizable as a man of virtue, endowed with a special kind of *pietas*, long before his messianic function becomes explicit. Piety and compassion temper the justice executed by Natty with his long rifle. When in *The Last of the Mohicans* a wounded Huron, finally weakening, slips from the tree on a cliff where he has been clinging, Natty, though surrounded by enemies, uses his last charge of powder to bring an instant death in mid-air, a far less horrible one than that awaiting on the rocks below. Earlier, when he is forced to shoot a human being for the first time, Natty (who is *The Deerslayer*) is tender and merciful to his dying enemy, a charity especially kind in view of the fact that the Mingo has, without provocation, twice tried to take Natty's life by treachery:

> . . . Deerslayer raised the Indian in his arms, and carried him to the lake. Here he first helped him to take an attitude in which he could appease his burning thirst; after which he seated himself on a stone, and took the head of his wounded adversary in his own lap, and endeavored to soothe his anguish in the best manner he could.

The whole chapter in which this incident occurs is rich with clues to Natty's character. A beautiful episode which introduces the youthful Deerslayer to the world's evil, bringing him to a man's estate and earning him a warrior's name, it is an unrehearsed ritual of initiation, one which, as several critics have noted, has been repeated with Twain's Huck Finn, Hemingway's Nick Adams, and Faulkner's Ike McCaslin. But there is something finer and more chivalric in Natty's induction into manhood than in that of any of those who followed. The innocence with which he enters the silent forest alone at dawn, the courage demonstrated when he is attacked, the refusal to strike when he has his opponent at a disadvantage, the compassion felt for his dying assailant, and finally, the regeneration he experiences at the conclusion of the ordeal, all render religious overtones suggestive of the quest of the pure in heart for the Holy Grail.

Surrounded daily by riches easily accessible to him—land, timber, furs—Natty renounces property as a poison to the soul. The love of money, he has discovered, is the root of at least some of the evil of the world, as he states in *The Pathfinder:*

> "I trouble myself but little with dollars or half-joes, but I can easily believe, by what I've seen of mankind, that if a man *has* a chest filled with either, he may be said to lock up his heart in the same box."

Evading the lure of wealth, Natty anticipates Thoreau's recounting, in *Walden,* of his gains from a farm near Concord: "I retained the landscape and . . . annually carried off what it yielded without a wheelbarrow." So Natty Bumppo in *The Pathfinder,* written more than a decade earlier, values the poet's claim to the countryside above the settler's title deed:

> "Now, here am I, a hunter and a scout and a guide, although I do not own a foot of land on 'arth, yet do I enjoy and possess more than the great Albany Patroon [Van Rensselaer]. With the heavens over my head to keep me in mind of the last great hunt, and the dried leaves beneath my feet, I tramp over the ground as freely as if I was its lord and owner; and what more need heart desire?"

(Critics of "Landlord Cooper" and the "American Aristocrat" would do well to remember that his greatest character creation was a man of property only in this highly imaginative sense.)

Natty also remains celibate throughout his life. In the first three *Tales* written, consideration of marrying never seems to occur to the mature scout, and he stays aloof from the dainty, fancily-dressed daughters of the British officers and American gentlemen. Not only does he consider himself socially inferior to them, but he shows no interest in becoming entangled in a way of life that would obligate him to possess a certain amount of property and a permanent home. He is equally disinterested in finding an Indian bride, for unlike many of the scouts and trappers who became "squaw men," Natty believes it against both nature and divine will to combine the races in marriage.

In the last two Leather-Stocking stories written, however, love takes on depth and gravity, and the scout himself is finally subject to truly deep feelings of love for a woman. In *The Pathfinder* Natty is nearly forty, but the young, pretty, intelligent Mabel Dunham now brings restlessness and yearning thoughts of domesticity to the formerly tranquil and solitary man. In a Dickensian interview between them, her confession that she does not share his feelings actually causes tears to fall down the rugged face of the usually stoic-demeanored scout. Although her father has desired and blessed their betrothal, Mabel prefers the younger, more lettered Jasper Western, and to his young friend Natty sorrowfully concedes his beloved. In Cooper's final *Tale,* which in story chronology predates *The Pathfinder,* appeals to marry come from both the pretty white girl Judith Hutter and the Huron woman who has been widowed, but the young Deerslayer summarily rejects them both. Mabel Dunham is thus his only love.

Natty is religious, but it is his natural piety, more than what he calls "missionary doctrine" inculcated by the Moravians, that sustains him in all his thoughts and actions, and causes him to see everywhere manifestations of a benevolent and divine will: "It is not easy," he says, "to dwell always in the presence of God, and not feel the power of his goodness." When challenged to cite chapter and verse from the book which supports one of his views, Natty scorns the written word and the presumptions to which it leads some men, favoring "nature's light" which teaches man humility. He states in *The Last of the Mohicans:*

> "I have heard it said that there are men who read in books to convince themselves there is a God. I know not but man may so deform his works in the settlement, as to leave that which is so clear in the wilderness a matter of doubt among traders and priests. If any such there be, and he will follow me from sun to sun, through the windings of the forest, he shall see enough to teach him that he is a fool. . . ."

At times he moves from this deistic path to one which approaches, but only approaches, pantheism. Exclaiming over the beauty of the still-virgin forests around Lake Glimmerglass, Natty sees Nature as a moral instructor, much as Wordsworth, and more recently Bryant, had before him. He tells Harry March in *The Deerslayer:*

> "This is grand!—'tis solemn!—'tis an edication of itself, to look upon . . . everything left in the ordering of the Lord, to live and die according to his own designs and laws! Harry, your Judith *ought to be a moral and well-disposed young woman, if she has passed half of the time you mention in the centre of a spot so favored."* (Italics mine)

Should the sensitive soul, ignoring such benign leadings, commit dishonest or shameful deeds, he will find the instructor turned monitor, threatening the conscience with feelings of guilt. As Wordsworth recounted in *The Prelude* the disapproval he sensed in Nature following his occasional acts of stealth, so Natty tells of similar admonitions. When, for example, Harry March fires wantonly at a deer whose flesh they do not need for food, Natty hears reproaches in the rolling echoes of the blast given back by the surrounding hills:

> "Them echoes are more awful in my ears than your mistake, Harry; for they sound like the voice of natur' calling out ag'in a wasteful and onthinking action."

But behind the Creation is a Creator, and Natty, never confusing the one for the other, views Nature as the house of the Lord, the only church in which he can worship satisfactorily. He explains in *The Pathfinder:*

> ". . . I have endeavored to worship garrison-fashion, but never could raise within me the solemn feelings and true affection that I feel when alone with God in the forest. There I seem to stand face to face with my Master; all around me is fresh and beautiful, as it came from His hand; and there is no nicety of doctrine to chill the feelin's. No, no; the woods are the true temple, a'ter all, for there the thoughts are free to mount higher even than the clouds."

As an American anchorite Natty communes daily in that true temple most of his long life, until the axes of the settlers desecrate its sanctity and he moves on to the plains. There he dies as devoutly as he had lived, standing literally face to face with his Master as he jumps to his feet and shouts cryptically "Here!" with his expiring breath.

His epitaph is spoken by a young woman of Templeton years after he has retreated westward from that fictional frontier village in central New York State. He is remembered in this area, says Eve Effingham in *Home as Found,* as "a man who had the simplicity of a woodsman, the heroism of a savage, the faith of a Christian, and the feelings of a poet. A better man than he, after his fashion, seldom lived." It was on this solid foundation of virtue that Cooper constructed the mythic hero of the *Leather-Stocking Tales,* "the most memorable character American fiction has given to the world," according to the *Cambridge History of American Literature.*

≈§ §≈

By the 1820's, when Cooper started to write about the Indian, there had accumulated a considerable body of lore about the red man—some of it indigenous to American life and thought, some of it the product of European social philosophers. Entering the symposium on the world's most celebrated aborigine at a relatively late hour, Cooper found the discussion already structured in terms of Primitivism and Anti-Primitivism. Wistful theorizing of European intellectuals of the eighteenth century such as Rousseau, Montesquieu, and Monboddo, and others even earlier, had established so strong an image of the Indian as noble savage that frontier realities over several generations had failed to obliterate its features. If settlers along the fringes of the forest knew better, urbanites along the seaboard still insisted in their poems and plays that many of the virtues to which the genteel aspired—honesty, kindness, sincerity, and faith—existed in their purest forms among the natives of America. To prove it, they cut out of the whole cloth of Primitivism Indian chiefs who not only exemplified these virtues but beyond that offered sage and eloquent counsel to their decadent white brethren. There had been a precedent for such red missionaries in English Georgian literature, and now they became an American staple. As hardheaded a realist as Benjamin Franklin could occasionally bring himself to indulge in fantasy about the noble red man, and for such pre-Romantics as Crèvecœur, Bartram, and Freneau, it took no effort at all. One example from Crèvecœur's *Letter from an American Farmer* illustrates the general tenor of their remarks:

Without temples, without priests, without kings, and without laws, they are in many instances superior to us; and the proofs of what I advance are that they live without care, sleep without inquietude, take life as it comes, bearing all its asperities with unparalleled patience, and die without any kind of apprehension for what they have done, or for what they expect to meet hereafter. What system of philosophy can give us so many necessary qualifications for happiness?

Factual prose accounts pictured inhabitants of quite a different sort lurking in the dark recesses of the wooded American wilderness. From the pages of journals, letters, and newspapers emerged creatures so fierce, so cruel, so bloodthirsty, and so depraved that

45

there seemed serious doubt about their membership in the family of man. Minions of the Devil some thought them, while others felt that they belonged to a less enlightened order, that of the wild beasts. Even as intelligent a man as Hugh Henry Brackenridge could refer to them as "the animals vulgarly called Indians."

Contributing heavily to this Anti-Primitivistic position were two types of repulsive-but-attractive stories: atrocity accounts, both accurate and embellished—home burnings, lootings, tortures, and massacres; and captivity narratives. The former were mainly of topical interest, disasters of the day, but the appeal of the captivity tale continued until it became a gruesome frontier classic. That one of these narratives, the account of Mary Jemison, the "Golden-Haired Seneca" as she was called, went through twenty-nine editions, the last in 1942, gives some indication of the popularity of such stories. Some idea of their number can be gained from the fact that the Ayer Collection in the Newberry Library, Chicago, has more than five hundred narratives, including variants, among its holdings; and a private library in Maine lists an even greater number.[1]

❧ ☙

Born with this background of romance, philosophy, and history, Cooper's Indians were unlikely to be recognizable copies of flesh-and-blood aborigines, even if he had attempted to copy them from nature. That he made, in fact, very little attempt to know them at first hand has now been generally agreed. There is agreement also, however, that the resulting medley of fact, fabrication, and folklore created one of the major nineteenth-century myths about America. Cooper achieved this by developing powerful images to symbolize both extremes of feeling about the red man: sentiment which converted the Indian into an exemplar of the fabled Golden Age, and horror which beheld in him little but animality and evil. It was these images, endowed with fictive life, that became the *dramatis personae* for the furious intraracial conflict which runs through all his Indian stories. Governor Cass would complain, on the one hand, that Cooper idealized his red men right out of the woods and into the missionary school of the Reverend John Hecke-

[1] Accounts of the Indians actually encountered in America, written in the seventeenth century by early missionaries and settlers, can be read in *Narratives of New Netherland* and other volumes of the ORIGINAL NARRATIVES OF EARLY AMERICAN HISTORY series, ed. J. Franklin Jameson (New York: Barnes & Noble, 1959).

welder (Cooper's chief source), while Francis Parkman, at the opposite pole, would shudder at realism occasionally so stark that it would "disgrace the shambles or the dissecting table" and make "ladies . . . regard his pages with abhorrence." But let the average reader suspend his disbelief for a moment only, and he is swept into a mythical world with its own set of values and its own inner reality.

Mohicans, Mohawks, Delawares, Onondagas, Hurons, Sioux, Pawnees, Wyandottés, Narragansetts, Wampanoags, Potawatamies are among the entries on Cooper's roster of Indian tribes, but they are, in many cases, little more than names. At times they may be rough indices of geography, revealing the approximate locale of the action; seldom do they designate real distinctions in aboriginal culture. Nearly all of Cooper's red men, regardless of tribe or tongue, are subsumed under the simple dichotomy—patently artificial even to lay readers and painfully naive to anthropologists—of "good" Indians and "bad" Indians. Only with reluctance does Cooper allow his villains to reveal occasionally some admirable quality, and he seems to praise with faint damns the savage traits of his nobler natives.

For the villains of his Leather-Stocking drama—and neither fairy tale nor Gothic romance chilled readers with more terrifying tyrants—Cooper selected from among the Iroquois peoples. Whether members of the Six Nations or of a tribe tributary to the Iroquois Confederacy such as the Hurons or Wyandottés, the Iroquois "Mingoes" are almost invariably the deadly foes of the protagonists. Perhaps they were well chosen for the role, these aborigines whom Parkman called the "Romans of the New World," and whose effective government and military prowess had made them in the sixteenth century the dominant force east of the Mississippi. Indeed, had Parkman viewed them through the eyes of conquered tribes he might have labeled them the "Huns of the New World," so fierce and unrelenting were they in some of their ways. Though no mention is made in the *Leather-Stocking Tales* of the cannibalism they reportedly practiced until as late as 1550, they are shown as little better than cave men, eating their freshly killed game raw! "Iroquois—devils—Mingoes—Mengwes—or furies," says Natty Bumppo at one point in *The Pathfinder*, "all are pretty much the same. I call all rascals Mingoes." For their own purposes, he and his creator alike certainly call all *red* rascals

47

Mingoes, and a more treacherous and bloodthirsty lot cannot be found anywhere in literature.

Juxtaposed with these Iroquois scourges of the wilderness are Cooper's well-known variants of the noble savage. They too, regardless of their tribal affiliation, come consistently from one major Indian family, the Algonquin. Whether presented at their best, as in the young Chingachgook and his delicate bride, or shown fallen on the hard times brought about by Iroquois domination, Anglo-Saxon invasion, and the white man's whiskey, the Algonquin Delawares and Mohicans are easily identified as the descendants of those ideal primitives who so often peopled the imaginations of eighteenth-century philosophers. Bravery, loyalty, self-sacrifice, and sentimental love confirm their direct lineage from those imaginary projections of the white man's better self, and whatever characteristics might betray ignobility within the framework of civilization are rationalized by Cooper in terms of cultural relativity as "red gifts." Reader sympathy for the protagonist is gained not only by the appeal of such attractive qualities, but, less positively, by the pathos of their fallen political state in the Iroquois-dominated Indian world.

In collecting material for his portrayal of the Delawares, Cooper turned to *An Account of the History, Manners, and Customs of the Indian Nations Who Once Inhabited Pennsylvania and the Neighboring States,* published in 1819 by the Reverend John Heckewelder, a Moravian missionary who for years had lived and worked among these people. Cooper found in Heckewelder's history the Delaware explanation of their own decline and fall as a power. At first only a rationalization demanded by tribal pride, the *apologia* acquired, with many years' retelling, such an air of authenticity that the missionary never doubted its accuracy. As the story was told to him in the lodges of the Sachems, the Delawares and Iroquois had once fought each other to a stalemate. Unable for once to conquer their opponents by force, the Mingoes resorted to trickery. They somehow persuaded the unsuspecting Delawares to accept Iroquois protection, abandoning military pursuits to become a nation of mediators for all Indian disputes in the East, and thereby benefactors of the whole race. Since only a few would be needed as mediators—these to be the ranking chiefs—the bulk of the Delawares were to pass their time in peaceful occupations, hunting and tilling the soil. They were, in Indian

48

terms, to assume the role of "women," no disgrace but a signal honor in a strongly matriarchal society unfamiliar with the white man's traditions. The offer was a magnanimous concession, supposedly, on the part of the then Five Nations (joined later by the Tuscaroras) to their former enemies. But once they had disarmed the enemy they could not defeat, according to the story, the Iroquois encouraged neighboring tribes to attack the defenseless Delawares until their numbers were decimated and their former power greatly reduced. Awakened to their predicament too late to effect a real recovery, isolated warriors of the Delawares struck back in hit-and-run guerrilla attacks on their oppressors.

It is a piece of pure folklore. Historians have demonstrated that the Iroquois had, in fact, decisively defeated on the warpath all their neighbors to the south in New York and Pennsylvania—Susquehannocks, Mahicans, Delawares—bringing them under the Confederation in the 1660's or 1670's, and had required them, in token of their subservience, to send north annual tribute in wampum. But the legend was precisely what Cooper needed to set the mood of his tragic myth. Doomed inevitably to final defeat, the heroic Delawares calmly demonstrate their nobility in the moral victories of unequal combat.

◅§ §►

The first of the *Leather-Stocking Tales* in story chronology, but the last written, is *The Deerslayer*. With the action set deep in the forest that white settlers were in the 1740's only beginning to invade, the novel is less complicated than are others by the problems of civilization. There is, in fact, an artistic limitation of time, place, and number of persons in this final work that allows both fuller characterization and more integration of character with setting and incident than some other volumes of the series demonstrate. Moreover, in Cooper's treatment of relationships between characters, and in his depiction of the scenic lake setting, there is a delicacy most appropriate to this story of youthful emotion and experience.

The best moments of the story involve Indian with Indian, including the adopted Delaware, Natty Bumppo. He and his Delaware companions, Chingachgook and Wah-ta-Wah, are all young, innocent as yet of the magnitude of evil in the world, and still susceptible to the pleasures of romantic sensibility. Opposing them, in a numerically superior force, is a party of Canadian Hurons, the Mingoes of the North.

The main action of the book is confined to a few June days on the waters and wooded shores of the serene Glimmerglass, clearly Otsego Lake, New York. The lovely Wah-ta-Wah, called Hist in familiar conversation, has been kidnapped from the Delaware camp by marauding Hurons; this situation has provided a just motive for Chingachgook, her betrothed, and Deerslayer, his friend, to go on (as the subtitle of the novel indicates) their "first warpath." Following different routes, the two youths overtake the Huron raiders on the shores of the quiet lake, where they ally with a pair of white renegades, Harry March and Tom Hutter, and Hutter's two daughters Judith and Hetty—all of whom Cooper fully develops as characters. Finally, with the additional aid of a scarlet-coated British regiment, Deerslayer and Chingachgook manage to retrieve the loved one, free themselves from captivity, and destroy the Huron band. Their first mission as warriors has been honorably accomplished.

That the Delawares are Cooper's "good" Indians would be immediately apparent even if the incorruptible Deerslayer were not their sworn brother. Their attractive representatives are the young lovers, innocent, devoted, and invariably dignified. Though only glimpses of their betrothment are seen, Chingachgook and Hist are as close to the sweethearts of sentimental fiction as their race's traditional reserve permits. What is left unspoken between them is lost only to the ear, for it is none the less understood and even more endeared in the language of the eyes. On the morning following her rescue, Hist joins Chingachgook on the boat's platform at dawn:

> The meeting between the two lovers was simple but affectionate. The chief showed a manly kindness, equally removed from boyish weakness and haste; while the girl betrayed in her smile and half-averted looks, the bashful tenderness of her sex. Neither spoke, unless it were with the eyes, though each understood the other as fully as if a vocabulary of words and protestations had been poured out.

Affection is also implicit in the pet names by which the lovers address each other. The young chief calls his forest maid "Honeysuckle of the Hills" and "Wren of the Woods," terms which are not merely convenient phrases of primitive gallantry but figurative expressions of real feelings. Even at a totally serious moment, when their very lives may be at stake, he develops one of these metaphors to tell her how earnestly he seeks her advice:

> "The smallest birds sing the sweetest; it is always pleasant to hearken to their songs. I wish I could hear the Wren of the Woods in my difficulty; its note would reach deeper than the ear."

Hist, in turn, calls Chingachgook by the names most cherished by a brave, his earned name, "The Great Serpent," and his patronymic, "Son of Uncas," the historical Uncases being among the greatest chiefs of the Algonquin peoples.

The only public avowal of their relationship, a long one, is spoken by Hist, not directly to Chingachgook but to Deerslayer. It is the answer, uttered with the rhythmical eloquence frequently attributed to American Indians, that Deerslayer is to carry back— a feat of memory for an unlettered hunter!—to the Hurons who are bargaining for her return to their tribe:

> "Among my people, the rose dies on the stem where it budded; the tears of the child fall on the graves of its parents; the corn grows where the seed has been planted. . . . Even the robin and the martin come back, year after year, to their old nests; shall a woman be less true-hearted than a bird? Set the pine in the clay, and it will turn yellow; the willow will not flourish on the hill; the tamarack is healthiest in the swamp; the tribes of the sea love best to hear the winds that blow over the salt water. As for a Huron youth, what is he to a maiden of the Lenni Lenape? He may be fleet, but her eyes do not follow him in the race; they look back toward the lodges of the Delawares. He may sing a sweet song for the girls of Canada, but there is no music for Wah but in the tongue she has listened to from childhood. . . . Wah-ta-Wah has but one heart, and it can love but one husband."

A sterner primitive virtue is the constant concern for honor, a concept relative *among* tribes but absolute *within* each tribe. On the warpath, every decision, every major move made by Chingachgook and Deerslayer is tested first in the crucible of tribal ethics. "Is this what a true Delaware would do?" they ask themselves. Or, viewed in terms of its effect on the group, will a given deed redound to the credit of the Delawares, when it is told at the council fires of the neighboring tribes, or will it be a cause for shame? Individual welfare is a consideration second to the good name of one's people, and Natty, faced with imminent death, is less worried about his own destruction at the hands of his Mingo captors than with the possibility that he might break during the torture and thereby disgrace his red brothers. Aware of Delaware integrity, Rivenoak, the Huron chief, allows Natty a day's reprieve from his ordeal, a "furlough," during which he is to act as messenger between the Hurons and the white settlers on the lake. The settlers, all of them morally inferior to most of the Indians, urge the hunter to disregard his promise to return. How ridiculous to die rather than break a promise made to a band of savages! When Judith Hutter urges this rationale of expediency upon Natty, he looks "at his fair questioner for a moment with stern displeasure," and then replies, "The Delaware would be the last man on 'arth to offer any objections to what he knows is a duty." It is not until the moment before his departure that he finally convinces her of the moral necessity of his return:

> "A furlough is a sacred thing among warriors, and men that carry their lives in their hands, as we of the forests do; and what a grievous disapp'intment would it be to old Tamenund, and to Uncas, the father of the Sarpent, and to my other fr'inds in the tribe, if I was to disgrace myself on my very first warpath. . . ."
> "I believe you are right, Deerslayer," returned the girl, after a little reflection, and in a saddened voice; "a man like *you* ought not to act as the selfish and dishonest would be apt to act; *you* must, indeed, go back. . . ."

Related to this ethic of tribal honor is loyalty to a brother, evidenced by Chingachgook's refusal to forsake the captive Deerslayer even though he is a lone Delaware against a score of Mingoes. To Natty's generous urging that he return home with his bride rather than attempt a rescue that would be virtual suicide, Chingachgook, quietly turning the tables, responds:

> "If Chingachgook was in the hands of the Hurons, what would my pale-face brother do? Sneak off to the Delaware villages, and say to the chiefs, and old men, and young warriors,—'See! here

52

is Wah-ta-Wah; she is safe, but a little tired; and here is the Son
of Uncas, not as tired as the Honeysuckle, being stronger, but just
as safe.' Would he do this?"

So conditioned are the Lenape by the strict code of their tribe
that they fear the retributive pangs of guilt that would surely follow such a cowardly act. Hist had earlier commented on the involvement of conscience in the matter:

> "Wah-ta-Wah says that neither she nor the Great Serpent could
> ever laugh again, or ever sleep without dreaming of the Hurons,
> should the Deerslayer die under a Mingo tomahawk, and they do
> nothing to save him. She would rather go back, and start on her
> long path alone, than let such a dark cloud pass before her
> happiness."

On the other hand, the Mingoes are guilty, if largely so off-
stage, of all the deviltry to which Cooper predestined them. "Rascals," "reptiles," "vagabonds," "wolves" are among the names
which Natty, by no means an Indian hater, applies to them. They
had killed Tom Hutter's only son, and three times they had burned
out the Hutter cabin, forcing the family finally to live on the water
in a house built on a reef and in an auxiliary floating home, a
scow they call "the ark"; it is an unprovoked Huron attack on
the ark that touches off hostilities in the novel. They are known
to take a morbid delight in torture as they "scalp, and cut, and
tear, and burn . . . until nothing is left but ashes," and indeed
they finally do scalp old Tom Hutter live. Chingachgook warns
Deerslayer that after his furlough he "will go back to the Hurons
to be treated like a bear that they roast and skin, even on a full
stomach." Their craftiness is proverbial—"cunning as a Mingo"—
and their treachery is exemplified in the warrior who fires at Natty
from ambush, shakes hands with the forgiving hunter in a peace
pact, and then tries to shoot him in the back as he trustingly departs. It is no wonder that the hero is forced to conclude, "It is
but a hopeless expectation to look forward to a Mingo's turning
away from evil and letting mercy get uppermost in his heart."

⇜ ⇝

The second volume of the Leather-Stocking story enforces the
contrast between the noble Delawares and the barbarous Mingoes.

In *The Last of the Mohicans,* which picks up the story of Chingachgook and Natty Bumppo some fourteen years later, the setting has shifted north to Glens Falls and the Lake George region, where the plot turns on a real historical event—the surrender of Fort William Henry to the French in 1757, with the subsequent Indian massacre of its British defenders despite Montcalm's assurance of a safe-conduct southward. But the introduction of historical facts does not eliminate melodrama. In fact there is more of it here as Natty, whose infallible shooting aim has now given him the name Hawkeye, is called upon to effect several rescues just in the nick of time; while ruses, disguises, and ambushes multiply in every quarter of a landscape crammed with hundreds, rather than tens, of lurking redskins. The killing of the innocent, perpetrated by both the Delawares and the Mingoes, is brutal—as when a mother and her baby are tomahawked, or an unsuspecting young Frenchman is scalped. Although the Indian is still the central figure, as the title indicates, it is noticeable that white actors are beginning to occupy more of the stage, as if emblematic of what was happening in the larger drama of colonial expansion. Attention is distracted from the main conflict by echoes of the sentimental novel found in the courtship of Major Heyward and Alice Munro, and by the antics of a comic Yankee, the psalmodist David Gamut. But either because of these extraneous elements or in spite of them, *The Last of the Mohicans* remains the most popular volume of the Leather-Stocking saga.

The Delaware and Mingo qualities are embodied in the opposing characters of Uncas, "the last of the Mohicans," and Magua, a crafty Huron villain. Uncas is the son born to Chingachgook by Hist, who now "slumbered beneath the pines of the Delawares." Although the geography suggests that he was probably a Mahican, *Uncas* was a family name among the Mohegans (a New England, not a New York tribe), and thus Cooper's *Mohicans* are a blend of two Algonquin tribes, the Mahicans of the Hudson River Valley and southeastern New York, and the Mohegans of Connecticut and Rhode Island. If Uncas was not the last of his people, he has nevertheless achieved enduring fame in the fictional forests where he lived and died. Moreover, he adds to the novel a dimension of romantic pathos never again quite reached in Cooper's novels.

Strong-bodied, agile, swift of foot, and graceful in all his movements, Uncas is represented as a specimen of the flawless physique "which abounds among the uncorrupted natives." He is a splendid figure, and frequent reference is made to his physical appearance:

> . . . his dark, glancing, fearless eye, alike terrible and calm; the bold outline of his high, haughty features, pure in their native red; . . . the dignified elevation of his receding forehead, together with all the finest proportions of a noble head, bared to the generous scalping tuft.

He has promise as a warrior—it is he who organizes and leads the Delaware forces in the final rout of the Hurons—but his first warpath becomes his last when he abandons prudence for chivalry in a vain attempt to rescue a white woman captive of the Iroquois.

Along with Chingachgook and Hawkeye, he is committed to protect Alice and Cora Munro during their trip to join their father, Colonel Munro, the commandant at Fort William Henry. In the course of their hectic journey, Uncas becomes attached to Cora, the mulatto daughter of the Colonel from his first marriage (with a West Indian girl of mixed blood). Contrary to the usual relationship between the sexes in Indian society—and Cooper evinces his awareness of this difference—the young chief is attendant upon all of Cora's needs,

> performing all the little offices within his power, with a mixture of dignity and anxious grace that served to amuse Heyward, who knew well that it was an utter innovation on the Indian customs, which forbid the warriors to descend to any menial employment, especially in favor of their women.

When Magua, also enamoured of the dark-skinned beauty, abducts her, with the aid of two Hurons, Uncas, beside himself, outdistances the rescue party he leads and engages the trio single-handed. Though fatally stabbed in the back, he manages to dispatch the Huron who, against Magua's orders, has killed Cora, and he dies stoically scorning the rage of Magua, as Magua maniacally slashes his body again and again.

Pathetic in itself, the death of Uncas symbolizes still greater pathos in the expiration of a noble family, and beyond that in the passing of a race. It is this greater significance of the Mohicans' loss which informs the epilogue spoken by the ancient Tamenund (Tammany, the same sachem who seventy-odd years before had welcomed Penn):

"Go, children of the Lenape, the anger of the Manitou is not done. Why should Tamenund stay? The pale-faces are masters of the earth, and the time of the redmen has not yet come again. My day has been too long. In the morning I saw the sons of Unamis [the turtle totem] happy and strong; and yet, before the night has come, have I lived to see the last warrior of the wise race of the Mohicans."

Magua serves not only as the arch-villain of the novel but also as one of the author's hedges against the oversimplification of "bad" Indians *versus* "good" Indians. To the Huron's villainy the reader cannot extend forgiveness, but he is forced to give some understanding. Automatically ferocious, by virtue of his kinship with the unregenerate Iroquois, Magua nevertheless reveals in flashes an innate bravery and dignity. His wildness, paradoxically, is made even more pronounced by his contact with civilization. The French had taught him to drink whiskey, and in its grip he had become so irresponsible that his own tribe, the Hurons, had finally banished him. Adopted by the fierce Mohawks, who at once suspected and admired him, he eventually became a scout for the English army, but his weakness for the white man's firewater continued to betray him, until finally one morning he reported to the English camp quite drunk. For this infraction of rules he was flogged, the commandant, Colonel Munro, understanding military discipline better than he did the workings of the Indian mind. The indignity of corporal punishment was never forgiven by the proud warrior. By the time the novel opens, his naturally savage character is twisted by the sufferings of exile and driven by the Indian demand for revenge. He despises nearly everyone, and his feelings even for Cora are ambivalent, attracted as he is by her charms, yet mindful of her relationship to the Colonel. Of all Cooper's Indians, none has chilled the blood or tingled the spines of more readers, young and old, than has Magua the Mingo.

The Indian-white alliances of the colonial wars between the French and British presented a real dilemma for Cooper when he came to write *The Last of the Mohicans*. Historically, the Iroquois supported the British, and his favored red men were on the side of the French. But Hawkeye, who was destined to become an actor in the great drama of the American frontier, could hardly fight alongside forces soon to be driven forever from the field, so he is found, together with his faithful red Achates, Chingachgook, and the latter's son, lined up as an ally of the British and the hated Mingoes. Their now official friends are still, however, their personal enemies, and they take turns cursing the Oneidas and Mohawks who cross their paths. When Hawkeye discovers that Heyward has employed a Mingo as guide, he growls

". . . they are a thievish race . . . you can never make anything of them but skulks and vagabonds. . . . I tell you that he who is born a Mingo will die a Mingo. . . . A Mohawk! No, give me a Delaware or a Mohican for honesty; and when they will fight . . . look to a Delaware, or a Mohican, for a warrior!"

With the Iroquois proper ineligible for villains' roles, Cooper substituted for them their Mingo cousins of the North, the Hurons, who in the novel provide France's Montcalm with many more warriors than they did in history. And then, lest the three Delawares of the Hills bear tomahawks against their own brothers, Cooper has the Delawares of the Lakes—northern kinsmen who *were* strong allies of the French, according to Heckewelder—refuse aid to Montcalm in the battle for Fort William Henry, on the flimsy pretext that they need more time to sharpen their hatchets.

◆§ §◆

With the retelling of the Indian myth in succeeding *Leather-Stocking Tales*, and in the other novels set in the American forests, there is essentially little that is added, but variations in the images of noble and ignoble red men strengthen the general impressions of their types. In *The Pathfinder* the traitor is a Tuscarora named Arrowhead, strongly reminiscent of Magua and again an Iroquois, as the Tuscaroras were the sixth of the Six Nations. Like the villain of *The Last of the Mohicans*, he leads into ambush the white party he is guiding and, like him, falls in love with one of the white girls. But he never attains the Satanic stature of Magua, and though his scalp is later added to Chingachgook's collection, in an isolated victory of red good over red evil, it is not with unrelieved loathing that the reader remembers him, and the sight of his gentle Indian wife, Dew-of-June, lingering to lament at his grave, tempers the repulsion one might have felt for him. Nor does the Delaware-Iroquois conflict in *The Path-*

finder, bloody as it is, assume the importance it previously had, as the freshwater seamanship on Lake Ontario, the suspicion of a traitor within the white party itself, and the heartaches of Natty, Mabel, and Jasper often dominate the story.

❧ ❧

By the time of *The Pioneers,* 1793, only thirty years removed from the time of its writing, merely an echo of the war cry is heard as Cooper recounts, in a passage of exposition, the history of the Eastern Delawares. Natty's rescues deliver victims from beast and fire, but no Indian ambushes threaten the quiet settlement of Templeton, identified by Cooper in his introduction to the novel as a representation in site, community structures, and "customs of the inhabitants" of early Cooperstown. Much of the book (which actually was the first *Leather-Stocking Tale*) is given to this fairly vivid depiction of the villagers' meeting places and their activities and excitements—such as the turkey shoot on Christmas Day—as they vary with the seasons.

The lone vestige of the intraracial conflict is Chingachgook, now old, alcoholic, and superficially Christianized under the name of John Mohegan, a mere mockery of the man who, as Natty tells some scornful bystanders, was "as comely a red-skin as ye ever set eyes on," and came back one day from battle with the Mingoes displaying thirteen reeking trophies on his scalp pole. Seemingly the red struggle must close with Chingachgook, as the old warrior, disavowing Christianity, dons battle garb and in an unreluctant death departs for the happy hunting grounds; but then in the final volume of the series it recurs some ten years later a thousand miles to the west.

❧ ❧

Pushing toward the sunset in *The Prairie,* the aged Natty, too feeble now to earn his living by hunting, is reduced to the level of a trapper, somewhere on the fringes of the Great Plains. There he encounters roving bands of Plains Indians and finds a place among them. It is Pawnees and Sioux who live on that part of the prairie, tribes with which Cooper reportedly had more contact than he had with some of the eastern Indians whom he portrayed. An acquaintance wrote that

"THE TURKEY SHOOT" FROM THE PIONEERS, OIL BY TOMPKINS H. MATTESON, 1857

Cooper followed a deputation of Pawnee and Sioux Indians from New York to Washington [D.C.], in order to make a close study of them for future use. He was much interested in the chief's stories of their wild powers, dignity, endurance, grace, cunning, wiles, and fierce passions.

In an introduction which she wrote for *The Prairie* his daughter Susan tells of the great interest with which he listened to "accounts of great buffalo hunts, of wild battles between mounted tribes, of fires sweeping over those vast plains." Substantial evidence has been collected to demonstrate that Cooper used the best authorities then available in his research on western Indians, drawing from the explorers Lewis, Clark, Long, Mackenzie, and Charlevoix both general impressions and such minutiae as names, expressions, topographical features, and local customs. For example, in the virtually sole interior scene of this outdoor drama Cooper takes the reader into one of the Sioux chief's own lodges. There, in a quiet, penetrating episode, he reveals the sorrow and humiliation suffered by the chief's youngest wife as she hears her husband, without a thought for her, address a new love as he had once courted her.

However accurately Cooper may have tried to picture these red horsemen of the Plains, one nonetheless senses in his Pawnees and their oppressors transmogrified Delawares and Iroquois. Even before the reader sees the Sioux in action, he is warned against them in terms similar to those Natty had used to curse the Mingoes: "red devils," "a dangerous and treacherous race," "Ishmaelites of the American desert." Their leader, Chief Mahtoree, like Magua, fulfills his nature in vainglorious conquest and gloating sadism, and yet he too elicits from the reader grudging admiration for his cool leadership and his total disregard of personal safety when the honor of his tribe is in question. It is more than personal pride which, when he has been fatally wounded, induces him to jump into the swirling waters of the river in a last desperate attempt to keep his scalp from drying in the tent of the Pawnee. Majestic in his villainy, he ranks at times with Milton's fallen angels. When he reconnoiters the poorly guarded camp of Ishmael Bush one night, for example, he enters by stealth, but then "raising himself on his feet, he stalked through the encampment, like the master of evil, seeking whom and what he should first devote to his fell purposes."

The fitting subjects of this Prince of Darkness are his stalwart Teton Sioux followers. When the Pawnee chief Hard-Heart rallies his outnumbered forces by exhibiting Mahtoree's scalp, claimed even from his watery grave, a hard core of "the most desperate braves still lingered nigh the fatal symbol of their honor, and there met their deaths." When the few remaining Sioux finally disperse, the aged chief Bohrecheena, mortally wounded, permits himself to be borne away by young Swooping Eagle only until he realizes that their double-mounted pony cannot possibly outrun the pursuing Pawnees. Then he immediately orders his youthful companion to halt, dismount, and kill him, there being no choice between death and dishonor.

> The old man raised his tottering frame to its knees, and first cast-ing a glance upward at the countenance of his countryman, as if to bid him adieu, he stretched out his neck to the blow he himself invited. A few strokes of the tomahawk, with a circling gash of the knife, sufficed to sever the head from the less valued trunk. The Teton mounted again, just in season to escape a flight of arrows which came from his eager and disappointed pursuers. Flourishing the grim and bloody visage, he darted away from the spot with a shout of triumph. . . .

In a day of defeat here was the consolation of a moral victory to clear the briars from Mahtoree's path to the eternal hunting grounds.

Alongside such lurid figures even their fellow red men must seem pale by comparison, especially the Pawnees, predestined by their author to virtue. Natty Bumppo not only assures the reader of their essential goodness ("A Pawnee is not apt to be a malicious savage") but when he has seen them prove their mettle in trials of both war and peace, he promotes them in his moral hierarchy of Indians to a position just short of perfection:

> "They are a valiant and an honest tribe," he said; "that will I say boldly in their favor; and second only do I take them to be to that once mighty but now scattered people, the Delawares of the Hills."

In Hard-Heart's refusal to unite with the Sioux to drive the white men back across the Mississippi, Cooper clearly suggests the his-torical role of the Pawnees as friends, scouts, and finally allies of the settlers. (Much later they even provided a famous battalion of guards to protect the Union Pacific Railroad against the sabotage of hostile tribes.) When Natty and Hard-Heart expect death at the hands of the Sioux, Natty lectures one of their less valiant captors: "Look at that Pawnee, Teton, and see what a Red-Skin may become, who fears the Master of life, and follows his laws." He may become an heir of the noble savage, and noble in many respects are the Pawnees among whom Natty Bumppo chooses to spend his last days.

The Prairie contains parallels to its predecessors other than that of the Indian dichotomy. Written immediately after *The Last of the Mohicans,* it is actually its sequel, despite the intervention in story chronology of *The Pathfinder* and *The Pioneers.* The young Middleton here is the descendant of Colonel Munro of *The Last of the Mohicans* and he bears the name Uncas in remembrance of the son of Natty's old friend Chingachgook. Just as the naive psalmodist David Gamut provides comic relief in the preceding book, so the naturalist Doctor Obed Battius creates real humor in *The Prairie* with his inappropriate Latin nomenclature for all persons and things, his obliging companion Asinus, and his fervent note-taking for the cause of science.

The Prairie also bears parallels to one of the *Tales* that was to follow its writing, *The Deerslayer.* Both works reveal selfishness and brutality on the part of white men; Ishmael Bush of *The Prairie* has been called one of Cooper's most memorable characters. And these three books all employ a stock motif of the romance, in that a young girl is kidnapped and the villains pursued by her lover.

❧ ☙

Nevertheless, the five *Leather-Stocking Tales* contain an internal chronological order, and when so arranged they reveal a symbolic strength that gradually declines and dies in both the solitary, skilled white scout and his Indian friend whose race is pushed westward and finally destroyed.

Admittedly, Cooper lacks realism in several aspects of these works and his prose is marked by the rhetoric of the nineteenth century, but it would be a mistake to deny the literary value of the novels. It is erroneous as well to equate the artistic qualities of the five books. It is noteworthy that three of the stories—*The*

Pioneers, The Last of the Mohicans, and *The Prairie*—were written between 1823 and 1827, and it was not until 1840 that Cooper wrote *The Pathfinder,* followed by *The Deerslayer* in 1841. Regarded in this sequence, as the series concludes Natty and Chingachgook grow younger and more forceful, and claim more of the author's attention; feeling intensifies and there are deeper relationships between characters; scenery becomes beautiful and focal. All of this makes distinct the separation between the two final volumes and the preceding three.

In the order of actual writing, also, the legend progressively becomes, not a dirge for the Indian and the scout who accompanied him, but a glorification of the red man and his companion in their wild and abundantly verdant world, where tribal pride, utter fearlessness, and individual skill credited a warrior, while reserve and total deference recommended a maiden.

Nonetheless, as time and age do not reverse, Natty Bumppo's historically symbolic career reveals its greatest significance only when the saga is followed realistically, in logical succession to its conclusion.

4

❦ THE GULL'S WAY

For twenty-five years Cooper wrote thorough-going nautical tales that move across the seven seas and through a variety of subjects. Structurally, most of them follow a pursuit-and-escape pattern for which Cooper exploits all the possible causes of hide-and-seek on the high seas: piracy, privateering, smuggling, spying, and treasure hunting. Only in *Mercedes of Castile* (1840), a historical romance which dramatizes Coiumbus' discovery of America, is the action contained by the gunwales of one ship, and then only out of necessity, the hero being supposedly "the first that ever burst into that silent" western sea. In all the rest it is either ship *versus* ship, with the skill of the respective crews competing for victory, or, as in the case of *The Two Admirals* (1842), fleet against fleet. The ship does not serve solely as a device to hold diverse characters in close contact where they are forced to make meaningful social and psychological adjustments; Cooper's yarns are thus not comparable to Conrad's *The Nigger of the Narcissus* or to Heggen's *Mister Roberts*. Whatever psychological drama may be enacted aboard ship, and often there are piquant conflicts of personality, the controlling narrative moves in a larger context.

Like Scott before him, Cooper used a wide range of historical settings for his fiction, the action of his sea tales spreading in time from 1492 with *Mercedes* to the 1840's with *Jack Tier* (1848). Even the epical climax of the earliest of these, Columbus' landing in the West Indies, fails to inject enough vitality into that book to make it exciting, and its mediocrity provides evidence toward the generalization that has already been made for all of Cooper's fiction: his best work is based on his own experience or on knowledge acquired through an oral tradition rather than on the dead data of a library. He is markedly more successful as he moves closer to his own era and the people he knew with *The Water-Witch* (1831). Textured with a wealth of realistic details, from folk talk to ship dimensions, the work would have a healthy vitality even without its thrilling subject: the elusive operations of a smuggler in the coastal waters off New York shortly after the end of Dutch rule in the colony. The modern critic Yvor Winters has been sufficiently impressed with "The Skimmer of the Seas," as *The Water-Witch* was often known (after its subtitle), that he rates it as Cooper's best:

> This novel, though imperfect artistically, is imperfect in minor ways; questions of scope aside, it is probably Cooper's ablest piece of work, as it is certainly one of the most brilliant, if scarcely one of the most profound, masterpieces of American prose.

In Cooper's own day the most popular of the sea tales were undoubtedly the two set during the American Revolution, *The Pilot* (1824) and *The Red Rover* (1828). The first of these heightens the already high romance of John Paul Jones's daring escapades during the war in much the same melodramatic manner that *The Spy* had earlier aggrandized the legend of Washington, but the truly memorable character creation of the work is an unlettered coxswain called Long Tom Coffin. The central figure of *The Red Rover*, an entirely fictitious hero-villain of Byronic proportions, moves from the British to the Patriot side by way of piracy, atoning for this unethical course in the end by losing his life gallantly to secure a naval victory for the Republic. With this sudden if unlikely character conversion, reminiscent of eighteenth-century sentimental comedy, the story was an inevitable choice for the theater, and the stage adaptation easily doubled its audience.

In several of the eleven sea tales contemporary America is home port. *Afloat and Ashore* (1844) and its sequel, *Miles Wallingford* (1844), compose a fictional biography of an Ulster County, New York, boy who goes to sea to seek his fortune, as Peregrine Pickle and Roderick Random had done before him; like Smollett's protagonists, Miles overcomes seemingly insurmountable obstacles to achieve worldly success and win the hand of the fair damsel who awaits his return. A signal difference is that while the actual adventures of Smollett's works occur almost exclusively on land, Cooper keeps his Horatio Alger action more afloat than ashore. *Homeward Bound* (1838), as the title suggests, describes a return trip from abroad, but it was a much longer trip, apparently, than the author had intended, as the *Montauk* sails from London to New York by way of Africa. Meant originally to be a social satire, it turned out instead to be a nautical prelude, as the voyage swept Cooper far off his course and took up an entire volume in itself before Captain Truck was able to outrun a British corvette, elude pirates, repair storm damage, and dock safely in New York. Perhaps *Jack Tier, or, The Florida Reef* is the most "realistic" of all Cooper's sea tales in the sense of presenting a morbid "slice of life." For moral decadence, for physical brutality on the part of supposedly civilized people, for moments of sheer horror, there is nothing like it anywhere else in Cooper's novels. Ostensibly a story of young love caught up unwillingly in the contraband trade during the Mexican War, it is remembered by the reader as a study of depravity in the person of Captain Spike and of pathetic, silent suffering in Molly Swash, his abandoned wife who follows him to sea in disguise as Jack Tier, cook and cabin steward. In Cooper's last American tale, *The Sea Lions* (1849), written only two years before his death, love conflict and religious conversion combine with melodramatic episodes—a quest for pirate gold, a seal hunt in the south polar seas, and a struggle for survival during an Antarctic winter—to make what Melville called "one of his happiest" works.

Less popular than his tales of American seamen are two novels set in European waters. *The Two Admirals* is the product of Cooper's long-postponed desire to manipulate whole fleets, instead of pairs of ships, and for once have not a *duellum* but a *bellum*. It is a story of that glamorous but quixotic rebellion in eighteenth-century England known as "The Forty-Five," in which Admiral

Bluewater, secretly a Jacobite, hesitates at a critical moment, undecided whether to support the main British fleet under his friend Admiral Oakes or to withhold his ships from action against the French allies of the Young Pretender. Friendship and the sense of duty finally overrule chauvinism and political theory, and Bluewater, to make up for his tardiness, throws his ships against the very center of the French line, saving the day for the House of Hanover but thereby losing his life. In *The-Wing-and-Wing* (1842) Cooper permits himself for once to favor the French sailor (elsewhere contemptuously called "Johnny Crapaud") as he traces the career of Raoul Yvard, a privateer for the Republic during the Napoleonic Wars. *Le Feu-Follet* (Will-o'-the-Wisp), or *Wing-and-Wing*, as the British call the ship because of her neatly balanced lugsails, flits about the Mediterranean preying on British shipping and collecting information about the movements of Nelson's fleet. Like the earlier Cooper ships *Water-Witch, Red Rover*, and Jones's frigate, it easily eludes all pursuers and might have done so indefinitely were the story a simple adventure. But, as he announced in the preface, Cooper, having himself become theologically quite conservative, wrote *The Wing-and-Wing* to set Deism and orthodox Christianity in contrast. Yvard, reared in France when the Age of Reason has sharply undercut Christianity, has fallen into "the error of the day," Deism, and when all pleas, even those of his beloved, fail to convert him, the Omnipotent (employing first the British Navy and then the sirocco) sends his light craft to the bottom bringing death to the stubborn heretic. But before orthodoxy demanded this punitive move, Cooper had enjoyed many a fine nautical maneuver aboard the trim little French lugger.

With these eleven novels and the secondary nautical elements in four of the land-based books, Cooper presented a whole panorama of the maritime world and charted a course for such successors as Melville, Conrad, McFee, and Forester.

៩ ៩

Although prose fiction from its very beginnings had drawn material from the marine world, as poetry before it had done since the time of Homer, the sea novel as a separate genre was not established until 1824 when Cooper published *The Pilot*. Literary history may point back to Defoe and Smollett, or to Barnabe

Riche, the retired Elizabethan sea captain who wrote adventure stories; one can even ferret out analogues and archetypes in the Greek romances of Heliodorus and Achilles Tatius of the third century B.C. Indeed the debt to earlier writers would be difficult to deny, especially in the matter of literary form. Here, as in most of his novels, Cooper leaned heavily on the fictional tradition of English romance writers for plot structure, conventions of heroic action, and formulas of escape-and-pursuit. But allowing the background its due, one can still say that Cooper was the creator of the sea novel as it is known today.

Augmenting the role of the sea itself was the most obvious innovation that Cooper made. Before his time, occasional scenes were set at sea, but they were invariably brief; in fact, most of the voyages of early sea fiction seem to have been made "between the paragraphs." The following chart suggests the greater shipboard emphasis of Cooper's most nautical novel compared with those of his three best-known predecessors in sea fiction, Defoe, Smollett, and Scott.

Author	Novel	Pages Total	Pages at Sea	Per-cent	Pages Describing Shipboard Life	Per-cent
Defoe	*Captain Singleton*	244	53	22	9	4
Smollett	*Roderick Random*	367	62	16.9	54	14.7
Scott	*The Pirate*	444	19	4	15	3
Cooper	*Homeward Bound*	532	526	99	309	58

Two single-sentence excerpts from DeFoe's *Captain Singleton* illustrate the sketchy fashion in which earlier novelists treated seamanship:

> "We continued our voyage south for many weeks, though with several intervals of going ashore to get provision and water."

Or again:

> "We sailed away for the Cape of Good Hope the beginning of October 1706 and passed by in sight of the Cape the 12th of November following, having met with a great deal of bad weather."

68

It took six weeks for Singleton to double the Cape, but as far as the reader is concerned, the journey might as well have been made in a prairie schooner as in a square rigger! So noticeably lacking from pre-Cooperian nautical tales are the numerous vignettes of the sea that might have given it a fictional life and character of its own.

Day by day, sometimes hour by hour, Cooper logs the details of weather and navigation. Before he permits the members of a ship's crew to go to their hammocks for the night or to set a fresh course in the morning, he accounts for their whereabouts and for the condition of the sea around them. A typical entry reads:

> The wind went down gradually, until there was little more than air enough to keep steerage-way on the vessel, while the ripple of the water disappeared, leaving nothing behind it but the long, heavy ground-swell that always stirs the bosom of the ocean, like the heaving respiration of some gigantic animal. The morning grew darker, but the surface of the gulf was glassy and tranquil, leaving no immediate motive for watchfulness or care.

In *Homeward Bound* there are over fifty separate notations of this sort on water and weather, some of them brief and others woven into the fabric of the action over the space of three or four pages.

There are tempestuous seascapes, too, in all of Cooper's nautical novels. By 1820 storms at sea had become a staple of romantic painting, and they had blown through the domain of romantic literature regularly since Childe Harold and Don Juan had thrilled at their fury. Cooper exploited the stock response they evoked, though he usually worked from factual accounts. In *The Sea Lions* the reader accompanies two ships beating round Cape Horn, which was always an ordeal in days of sail, for there the seas ran high and the wind blew steadily "in an Irishman's hurricane"—as the old salts phrased it—straight up and down! Cooper writes:

> The seas that came down upon the cape resembled a rolling prairie in their outline. A single wave would extend a quarter of a mile from trough to trough, and as it passed beneath the schooner, lifting her high in the air, it really seemed as if the glancing water would sweep her away in its force. . . . It was the current that

menaced with the greatest danger, for that . . . was clearly setting the little craft to leeward, and bodily toward the rocks. . . .
Could the deepest bellowing of ten thousand bulls be united in a
common roar, the noise would not have equalled that of the hollow sound which issued from the sea as it went into some cavern
of the rocks. Then, the spray filled the air like driving rain, and
there were minutes when the cape, though so frightfully near, was
hid from view by the vapor.

It is worth noting that two of Cooper's successors in sea fiction
recalled being deeply moved by such passages as these. Melville,
in reviewing *The Sea Lions* for the New York *Literary World,*
said of Cooper's treatment of the Antarctic seas, "Few descriptions of the lonely and terrible, we imagine, can surpass the
grandeur of many of the scenes here depicted." Later, Joseph Conrad paid Cooper the fullest compliment of a fellow author:

> He loved the sea and looked at it with consummate understand-
> ing. In his sea tales the sea inter-penetrates with life; it is, in a
> subtle way, a factor in the problem of existence, and, for all its
> greatness, it is always in touch with the men, who, bound on er-
> rands of war or gain, traverse its immense solitudes. His descrip-
> tions have the magistral ampleness of a gesture indicating the
> sweep of a vast horizon. They embrace the colours of sunset, the
> peace of starlight, the aspects of calm and storm, the great lone-
> liness of the waters, the stillness of watchful coasts.

If the general reader can understand Cooper's periodic reports
on the elements, only the initiated can appreciate fully his descriptions of ships and their gear, and his step-by-step account of
sailing operations. The landsman who is interested in sharing vi-
cariously the activities of the crew is frequently sent scurrying
below for a marine dictionary in order to fathom first the technical terminology employed. How otherwise could he be certain
about the exact function of a *bobstay,* a *carling,* a *garnet,* a *kedge,*
or a *rullock?* Or how could he be certain about what was to
transpire when orders were issued to *clew, luff, trice,* or *ware?*
Even Cooper's contemporaries, to whom sailing vessels were a
means of transportation and not merely the playthings of the
leisure class, must have experienced some mystification. But it was
only a particularly knowledgeable person who could find any

flaws in Cooper's seamanship and protest, as one English friend did after hearing a chapter of *The Pilot* read aloud, "It's all very well, but you have let your jib stand too long, my fine fellow."

Cooper recognized, of course, that many of the surface details of the sea novels must inevitably confuse some of his readers, and he created for *The Red Rover* a personification of this confusion in the comic figure of Widow DeLacey. Quite unaware that in her nautical education she has been carefully mistaught by her late husband, an admiral with a perverted sense of humor, she entertains the crew of the *Rover* on every new tack with her erring comments:

> "What natural object is there, or can there be," exclaimed the nautical dowager in a burst of professional enthusiasm, "finer than a stately ship breasting the billows . . . its taffrail ploughing the main, and its cut-water gliding after, like a sinuous serpent pursuing its shining wake."

This is funny, in its crude way. But the laughter of the readers is probably hesitant and uneasy, for they realize that they could be duped almost as readily as was the unsuspecting relict of the admiral.

This is not to imply that Cooper deliberately obscured his meaning or that he was reluctant to explain the mysteries of the seaman's trade for fear of profanation. As often as he could, without turning his novels into beginner's manuals, he enlightened landsmen in the audience on the ways of the sea. One such interpolation occurs in *Homeward Bound* when Cooper explains the elementary problems of *scudding,* or sailing before the wind; here, as usual, the professional terms are illuminated partly by explicit definition and partly by the context in which they appear (italics of nautical terms mine):

> The hazards now to be avoided were those of the ship's *broaching-to* or being *pooped.* Nothing may seem easier . . . than to "sail before the wind," the words having passed into a proverb; but there are times when even a favoring gale becomes prolific of dangers, that we shall now briefly explain.
>
> The velocity of the water, urged as it is before a tempest, is often as great as that of the ship, and at such moments the *rudder* is useless, its whole power being derived from its action as a mov-

ing body against the element in comparative repose. When ship and water move together, at an equal rate, in the same direction, of course this power of the *helm* is neutralized, and then the *hull* is driven much at the mercy of the winds and waves. Nor is this all; the rapidity of the billows often exceeds that of a ship, and then the action of the *rudder* becomes momentarily reversed, producing an effect exactly opposite to that which is desired. . . . In the present instance, the *Montauk* would seem to fly through the water, so swift was her progress; and then as a furious surge overtook her in the chase, she settled heavily into the element, like a wounded animal. . . .

Pooping is a hazard of another nature, and is also peculiar to the process of *scudding.* It merely means the ship's being overtaken by the waters while running from them, when the crest of a sea, broken by the resistance, is thrown *inboard,* over the *taffrail* or *quarter.* The term is derived from the name of that particular portion of the ship. In order to avoid this risk, *sail* is carried on the vessel as long as possible, it being deemed one of the greatest securities of *scudding* to force the *hull* through the water at the greatest attainable rate. In consequence of these complicated risks, ships that sail the fastest and steer the easiest, *scud* the best. There is, however, a species of velocity that becomes of itself a source of new danger; thus exceedingly sharp vessels have been known to force themselves so far into the watery mounds in their front, and to receive so much of the element on their decks, as never to rise again. This is a fate to which those who attempt to sail the American *clipper* without understanding its properties are peculiarly liable. On account of this risk, however, there was now no cause of apprehension, the *full-bowed, kettle-bottomed Montauk* being exempt from the danger. . . .

Detailed and lengthy as it is, this exposition is handled so skillfully that the reader never forgets its relevance to the action of the novel.

More important than the extent to which his audience was, or is, familiar with the nautical equipment of the novels is the fact that Cooper carried this paraphernalia of the sea over into fiction. Just as one sees much more blue water in his works than was visible in earlier stories, so one encounters ships in greater numbers and in more diverse shapes. Dozens of different craft ply Cooper's seas: warships of all sizes and descriptions—seventy-four-gun battleships, cruisers, frigates, armed sloops, corvettes; regular merchantmen—schooners, square-rigged brigs, and neatly balanced luggers; specially constructed vessels—trim London packets, sleek clipper ships, lateen-rigged feluccas, double-ended proas, light caravels, and short stubby whalers. Once aboard his ships, the reader mans the capstans, reefs the sails, and ducks as the boom swings past on every new reach; he sees, hears, feels, and occasionally even smells the same things that crew and passengers do. The net result is a dimension of which Smollett was incapable and Scott quite ignorant.

ⅇ⸱ ⸱ⅇ

Cooper's seamen are not, for the most part, such innovations in fiction as are the very real ships they operate and the real seas upon which they sail. Many of his sailors were, in fact, already familiar figures to readers by 1823. Some were re-dressed, freshly oriented members of Scott's and Byron's brigades; others had obviously been shanghaied from the still older crews of Smollett. A few, however, were original creations, characters whose component features perhaps had some precedence in men Cooper had known but whose total personalities he heightened until they became the beaux ideals of a new type of seaman. All together, over fifty of Cooper's seamen are sufficiently important to the tales in which they appear to earn from him individual portraits and thus become distinguished from the other characters, those nondescript clusters of humanity he vaguely refers to as "the ship's people."

Among the more particularized group, those closest to the heart of their creator were the "old salts," the rude, untutored men of the sea, like his good friend Ned Myers whose somewhat embroidered autobiography he published in 1843. By the time Cooper began depicting him, the old salt was very old indeed. A familiar folk type among a maritime people, he had early found a place in English literature. Although he appeared in print even before the Elizabethan period, it was then that he first made his presence felt, and after a number of successful roles in Restoration and eighteenth-century drama he became a stock figure. He was, thus, already a fairly well-defined type when Smollett came along and immortalized him in the persons of Bos'n Pipes, Lieutenant Hatchway, and Commodore Trunnion in *Peregrine Pickle* and in Tom Bowling in *Roderick Random*.

The old salts were honest, blunt, uncomplicated souls with "hearts of oak" who, in their own proverbial words, "earned their money like horses and spent it like asses." Underfed, overworked, exploited, they shipped for a voyage, blew their earnings on second-rate liquor and third-rate women, and then in desperation shipped again. An occasional tar had a family ashore toward whose support he contributed from his meager pay, but most of them were social derelicts. If the average mariner of the forecastle eluded the dangers and endured the hardships of the seafaring life until old age, he might retire to the snug harbor of a seamen's home or become a semi-active domestic in the household of some charitable person of means. Wherever he went, the old salt bore indelible earmarks of his calling. Besides displaying to the world a hearty sincerity (frequently contrasted with the affectation of landbound fops), he always walked with a roll and a lurch, hitched his trousers or shifted his quid for emphasis, and spouted an oath-filled, salt-water lingo on any and all occasions. Exaggerated by playwrights and novelists, he nevertheless had his real-life models discernible in every port. These were the tag characters of the sea, the "damn-my-eyes tars," as Melville was later to call them, who sailed from the English literary tradition into the fictional world of James Fenimore Cooper.

Many of them remained quite conventional, even to being named after parts of the ship or pieces of the rigging—Boltrope in *The Pilot,* Ben Pump in *The Pioneers,* and Galleygo in *The Two Admirals.* But others departed from the conventional type, no surprise to one acquainted with Cooper's background and the times in which he wrote. In the light of his own love for the sea, his favorite creations could hardly be indifferent to it; a child of the Romantic movement, Cooper must transmit to his literary progeny an awe for the wonder of things. And so the Cooperian salts, shaped by this heritage and launched into a new maritime world, became the prototypes of those romantic devotees of the deep, the sea-haunted heroes of Melville and Conrad.

In *The Pilot* and its successors one is made aware for the first time in prose fiction of a relationship between man and sea that transcends mere physical proximity. When the sailors of Defoe, Smollett, Scott—or of the playwrights, for that matter—think of the sea (something which they rarely do), they almost always think of it as a vast business site or as a road on which to seek their fortunes. They may own all or part of a vessel on which they sail, and evaluate each venture purely in terms of profit and loss; or they may join the company of a ship, naval or merchant, taking the best position for which they can qualify, and think of a voyage as simply a time unit in their life's occupation; or, finally, they may, for want of a better plan, go to sea in the vague and Micawberish hope that there "something will turn up" to bring them prosperity. But who among them is drawn from dry land by "a wild call and a clear call that may not be denied"? Certainly not Smollett's crews, for despite their salty speech and their maritime manners, they all eventually retire to the shore, never making the slightest effort to sail again, even in a pleasure craft. How many of them feel the mystery, the glamour, the challenge of the deep? How many of them are capable of that fervid appeal of Conrad's Marlowe:

> "Tell me, wasn't that the best time, that time when we were young at sea; young and had nothing on the sea that gives nothing, except hard knocks—and sometimes a chance to feel your strength—that only that you all regret?"

It is this kind of emotional response to the sea, whatever its specific motivation, which informs the sea novel in Cooper's hands.

We see it in Cooper's very first sea dog, Long Tom Coffin in *The Pilot*. As romantic a figure as ever trod a deck, he boasts kinship with what was probably the greatest seafaring family in American maritime history, the Coffins of Massachusetts, who by Cooper's time were already legendary in a dozen ports along the East Coast. It was they who dominated Nantucket, long the whaling capital of the New World, and when the industry moved to New Bedford and finally back to its birthplace in old Sag Harbor, it was with Coffins in the vanguard; it was a Coffin too who was responsible for the establishment of that curious inland whaler's base 125 miles from the sea at Hudson, New York. Tom is not exaggerating when he says:

> "Ay, Coffin . . . 'tis a solemn word, but it's a word that passes over the shoals, among the islands, and along the cape, oftener than any other. My father was a Coffin, and my mother was a Joy; and the two names can count more [whale] flukes than all the rest in the island [of Nantucket] together."

Less than thirty years after the publication of *The Pilot,* Herman Melville would have his Ishmael eat at Peter Coffin's Spouter Inn

75

and would cite Captain Charley Coffin as one of his authorities on the leviathan.

Passing his whole life at sea, Tom is an aquatic creature who flounders about, anxious and insecure, whenever he is forced to set foot on dry land.

> "Give me plenty of sea-room and good canvas, where there is no occasion for pilots at all, sir. For my part, I was born on board a chebacco-man [a type of vessel used on Newfoundland fishing banks], and never could see the use of more land than now and then a small island to raise a few vegetables, and to dry your fish. I'm sure the sight of it always makes me feel uncomfortable, unless we have the wind dead offshore."

Finally, when at a critical moment the winds conspire to blow shoreward, and his only home, the *Ariel,* is brought up on the reef of a lee shore, Long Tom pushes the youthful skipper into the last life boat to pull away and calmly goes down with the stricken vessel:

> "God's will be done with me. . . . I saw the first timber of the *Ariel* laid, and I shall live just long enough to see it turn out of her bottom; after which I wish to live no longer."

His is no mere drowning, but a symbolic return to "that immortal sea which brought us thither," and to suggest this Cooper translates Tom directly to the realm of the sea gods. In the wreckage that washes up on the beach everything and everyone is accounted for but Tom's body. It is never seen again, and as the survivors move off the scene they observe that "the sea was never known to give up the body of the man who might be emphatically called its own dead." Thus ends, in a fitting manner, the career of the first romantic old salt.

Long Tom has his counterparts in such other Cooperian tars as Moses Marble in *Afloat and Ashore,* Mr. Monday and Captain Truck in *Homeward Bound,* Stimson in *The Sea Lions,* and Charles Cap in *The Pathfinder.* The most voluble of these and the only active sailor in the Leather-Stocking series, Charles Cap, is like a stranded porpoise when he journeys inland to western New York to visit his brother. He complains:

"This is the worst of the land; it is all the while in motion, I tell you, though it looks so solid. If you plant a tree and leave it, on your return from a three years' v'y'ge, you don't find it at all the sort of thing you left it. The towns grow, and new streets spring up; the wharves are altered; and the whole face of the earth undergoes change. Now a ship comes back from an India v'y'ge just the thing she sailed, bating the want of paint, wear and tear, and the accidents of the sea."

The sea's face suggests eternity, and men gazing long upon it hold steadfast to their elemental faith; not so the landsman, avers Cap:

"Even religion on land isn't moored in exactly the same place it was in my young days. They veer and haul upon it ashore, as they do on all other things, and it is no wonder if now and then they get jammed. Everything seems to change but the compass, and even that has its variations. . . . Religion at sea is just the same thing that it was when I first put my hand into the tar-bucket. No one will dispute it who has the fear of God before his eyes."

The deep may have its perils, but the soul of man founders not so readily there as on the terrestrial portions of the globe. Salvation lies somewhere in the offing. A green deck hand with the voice of a poet, Ishmael in *Moby Dick,* would soon be saying the same thing in a different way, and with implications even more symbolic:

". . . as in landlessness alone resides highest truth, shoreless, indefinite as God—so better is it to perish in that howling infinite than be ingloriously dashed upon the lee, even if that were safety."

And so, in their respective ways, would all the future old salts of literature try to explain the meaning of the sea and the hold it had upon them.

But some of his intimations of the supernatural the seaman drew from the darker side of the spiritual world. He was more superstitious than the average person probably is, but understandably so. As Cooper points out in *Jack Tier:*

Sailors have been, from time immemorial, more disposed than men of their class on land, to indulge in this weakness [superstition], which is probably heightened by the circumstance of their living constantly and vividly in the presence of powers that menace equally their lives and their means, without being in any manner subject to their control.

Furthermore, his trade, essentially unchanged for centuries—this was before the age of steam—had always depended for its perpetuation on the oral transmission of nautical know-how, and along with the ways of the sea and of ships came, gratuitously, a considerable body of folk belief.

In a world where chance seemed to play a large part, it was only natural for seamen to attribute many of their experiences to the influence of good or bad luck. Through no merit or fault of their own, some sailors seemed to have an affinity for good luck, while others, like Hemingway's Santiago, suffer an extended run of luckless days. Thus, Daggett, Cooper's competent captain of the *Sea Lion* from Martha's Vineyard, has all sorts of mishaps— a broken leg, a jammed ship, and finally death for himself and his crew in the frozen Antarctic—and much of this must remain unaccounted for unless Dame Luck can be blamed. Other men made their own bad breaks by violating nautical taboos. They might make the mistake of taking aboard a Jonah, some evil person whose sins would bring down retribution on their heads as well as on his own. The crew of the *Ariel* is convinced it has made this mistake in carrying to sea as hostage the villain of *The Pilot,* Christopher Dillon; the ferrymen of the *Winkelried* in *The Headsman,* caught in a storm on Lake Geneva, are sure there is a Jonah aboard, and when they discover that among the passengers is the hereditary state headsman of Switzerland, a gruesome character in the eyes of the public, they fasten upon this unfortunate person as a fitting scapegoat.

To whistle in the wind was another way to invite bad luck, for it was almost certain to draw the fury of the elements. Long Tom gives this belief a religious twist when he explains it to a younker:

> "I know, from having followed the seas my natural life, that singing in a gale is sure to bring the wind down upon a vessel the heavier; for He who rules the tempest is displeased that man's voice shall be heard when He chooses to send his own breath on the water."

But perhaps the surest way to bring disaster for any undertaking was to begin it on Friday. Rather than weigh anchor for a voyage on Friday, it was better to lay over a day. In a footnote to *The Red Rover* Cooper records the outcome of a disbeliever's conflict with the force that gives rise to this superstition. In his *auctor dicit* he writes:

> The superstition, that Friday is an evil day . . . prevails, more or less, among seamen, to this hour. An intelligent merchant of Connecticut had a desire to do his part in eradicating an impression that is sometimes inconvenient. He caused the keel of a vessel to be laid on a Friday; she was launched on a Friday; named "The Friday"; and she sailed on her first voyage on a Friday. Unfortunately for the success of this well-intentioned experiment, neither vessel nor crew were ever again heard of!

Where Cooper found this information he does not reveal, but since it appears in one of his ordinarily factual commentaries, one must credit its authenticity until it has been disproven. In the passage of the novel itself the voice of the anti-folk attitude, as it so often is in Cooper, is the scornful voice of a Yankee; and significantly, the inherited wisdom of the folk proves to be superior to the Yankee's acquired learning.

Some of the seamen's lore found in Cooper's novels was later to be employed by Herman Melville, notably in *Moby Dick*. Common to the sailors of both writers is a belief in the finality of the third effort to accomplish something after the first two attempts have failed—an early form of the modern superstition "Three times and out." (Three is considered a very potent number, of course, and has a long history of its own in the province of magic.) In Cooper's *The Wing-and-Wing* an old seaman advises the skipper that it is pointless to pursue farther the predatory privateer they have hunted thrice in vain:

> "I never knew a craft found after a third look for her. Everything seems to go by thirds in this world, sir; and I always look upon a third chase as final."

With much the same foreboding, Starbuck of *Moby Dick,* filled with misgivings just before the beginning of the final day of the chase, reminds himself, in a passage of internal dialogue, of "this the critical third day":

> "For when three days flow together in one continuous intense pursuit, be sure the first is morning, the second the noon, and the third the evening and the end of that thing—be that end what it may. Oh! My God! what is it that shoots through me, and leaves me so deadly calm, yet expectant—fixed at the top of a shudder!"

A curious piece of death lore was common to the beliefs of the older crewmen of Cooper's fleet and the whalers aboard Melville's *Pequod.* It credits sharks with the ability to sense instinctively the approaching death, sometimes long ahead of time, of any creature whose carcass might provide food. They could detect imminent death aboard a vessel at sea, and they would follow in the wake for days waiting for an ocean burial. Little wonder that the flash of a fin off the stern of a windjammer was a cause for alarm. In five of Cooper's sea novels, from the first to the next to the last, this unexplained foreknowledge of death is attributed to sharks. Likewise, on that fateful third day of Ahab's running battle with Moby Dick, the sharks follow his whale boat as it pulls away from the ship, and in vain does a terrified crewman, reading the omen correctly, shout from the cabin window to the departing captain, "The sharks! the sharks! O master, my master, come back!" Ishmael, commenting upon the incident, remarks that these voracious fish lurked about "in the same prescient way that vultures hover over the banners of marching regiments in the east"; and then, as if to leave no doubt as to their import at this juncture, he adds, "These were the first sharks that had been observed by the *Pequod* since the White Whale had been first described."

Neither the men nor the ships that founder in the deep can be certain of resting peacefully "under the whelming tide." Drowned sailors were thought to haunt the area in which they had lost their lives, and their voices could often be heard before the gathering storm. At one point in *The Pilot,* Long Tom makes an escape along the British coast when the seamen guarding the beach think they hear the call of drowned mariners and withdraw from the water's edge in fear. Once again, Melville corroborates the authenticity of Cooper's sea lore by employing this same belief in *Moby*

Dick. The people of the *Pequod* hear plaintive cries from the water on the night before they meet the *Rachel,* only to learn next day that that vessel had recently lost a boatload of its crew in the immediate vicinity.

Sunken vessels rise again and ride the main in the folklore of many different peoples, and the ghost ships sighted from the foretops of Cooper's fleet certainly are not literature's first. One could even legitimately question whether his spectre ship lore was taken directly from the oral tradition or whether it was not rather borrowed from the many recorded accounts of nautical wraiths available to him. One could point to literary sources for tales of *The Fying Dutchman,* whose skipper haunts the high southern latitudes, living out the terms of his curse and trying in vain to beat around the Cape of Good Hope. Surely Cooper would have known these tales even if he had never bunked in a ship's forecastle, but there is every likelihood that he also heard them at sea. There is no reason to believe that the legend of *Die fliegende Holländer* disappeared from the oral tradition once it found a place in literature. Thus, unless one would accuse Cooper of inconsistency in the otherwise consistent portrait of Long Tom Coffin, it is good evidence for his having used folk sources that that illiterate seaman believes in The Dutchman as a part of the gospel of the sea. It is, he says, "what every man who has ever doubled Good Hope knows to be true," and though he himself has not sighted the cursed craft and her spectre crew, never having sailed below the Dark Continent, he has known "them that have seen her, and spoken her, too."

There are many other ghost ships afloat as well, and the ocean with which Cooper was best acquainted, the North Atlantic, has more than its share of them. Off the northeast coast of North America no fewer than fifteen phantom ships have been reported, some of them sighted even in this century, but most of them dating from the seventeenth and eighteenth centuries. It is psychologically realistic, then, that Cooper's sailors are wary of unidentified vessels or those which act at all strangely, and realistic too that they are often hasty to infer the presence of supernatural agencies in such craft.

As early as the opening chapter of his first sea novel Cooper employs the folk belief in ghost ships, and manages to do it in a most convincing way. Just before a storm, an ominous time, a pair of peasants on the English coast view two vessels that have loomed up suddenly, as if out of nowhere, sailing easily and un-harmed among the treacherous reefs just offshore. After some de-bate between the awe-stricken rustics, the two ships are pro-nounced to be "bogles of the saa." It augurs no good for those to whom such wraiths appear:

> "Ill luck bides o' some o' ye. Twa craft a sailing without hand to guide them, in sic a place as this, whar eyesight is na guid enough to show the dangers, bodes evil to a' that luik thereon."

And so the two leave the scene, never to reappear in the novel—but they have served their purpose well. It is a dramatic way to introduce the frigate and her schooner escort, and yet it is ap-propriate, too, for these are the ships of the fabulous John Paul Jones, a naval commander whose feats of daring were so uncan-nily successful that they seemed to many observers to transcend what was humanly possible. The warship, along with its tender, might well seem to the peasants to be a supernatural vessel, for in it the lone marauder who became the scourge of the British coast effected his escape time and again from the traps of the English Navy by the skillful navigation of shallows ordinarily impassable to vessels of that draught.

It should be noted that in *The Pilot* as well as in the other nov-els in which Cooper uses spectre lore, it is always just the *sug-gestion* of supernatural agencies with which one is confronted, not the actual presence. Unlike some writers who use the super-natural, Cooper never taxes his reader's credulity by asking him to believe in the impossible. He leaves that to folk characters who are themselves convinced of the operation of otherworldly forces and can thus quite realistically, within the framework of the novel, insist on the validity of these beliefs. To the person who sincerely believes he has seen a ghost, the apparition is as "real" as any of his other experiences, affecting him, perhaps, both men-tally and physically. Thus can dreams and illusions be made to contribute to the realism of a piece of fiction.

◆§ §◆

One of Cooper's own psychological substitutes for "going down to the sea again" was writing about it, and the nautical novels

The Bettmann Archive

ILLUSTRATION ACCOMPANYING EARLY EDITION OF COOPER'S
HISTORY OF THE NAVY OF THE UNITED STATES OF AMERICA

comprise only half of his work in this area. For he also became a
naval scholar, an unofficial historian of the Navy and a champion
of American sea power. In 1834 when he was invited to join the
U. S. Naval Lyceum, a New York City group interested in pro-
moting the service, he wrote back immediately:

> I beg to inform the gentlemen of the Lyceum of my acceptance
> of the compliment they have been pleased to confer on me. I have
> the more pleasure in this election, because it comes from a corps
> to which I once belonged myself, which I have always loved, and
> which has conferred so much credit on our common country.

In the *Naval Magazine,* for which he outlined a detailed program
for building into an effective force the country's small but strug-

gling Navy, he promoted the service with all the conviction of a career sailor. He wrote:

> The Navy can be made the most efficient means for maintaining the national rights, and the national character, that the people possess; it can be made a means of defence that no other power would presume to despise, or, within our waters, would presume to brave; it can easily and ought to be made to give us as absolute command of the North Atlantic ocean as England has ever had over her own narrow seas. . . .

In 1839 Cooper brought out, in two volumes, his monumental *The History of the Navy of the United States of America*. It was to remain unchallenged as the definitive work on the early history of the Navy until the twentieth century, and it is still a standard reference work. It is an extremely careful work, and if it at times seems colorless, it is so because Cooper scrupulously avoided the temptation to let the potential melodrama of his material develop. The novelist in him never encroached on the scholar; he did not confuse fact with fiction, history with legend. To the recollections of his own experiences at sea and the information provided by the many high-ranking officers among his friends, Cooper added voluminous data that he amassed by diligent research in the various annals of the Navy. His procedure was to sift through all this material, study it carefully and impartially, and then write the history as he believed the events had occurred, without slanting or heightening of effect. He refused to take sides, for example, in the furious and bad-tempered debate that had been raging for twenty years over the behavior of Oliver Perry during the Battle of Lake Erie; he commented only that the Commodore's celebrated transfer from his disabled flagship to the *Niagara,* in an open boat under fire at the height of the battle, was "the least of Perry's merits." But the Perry clan, expecting a eulogy for their hero and a sharp rebuke for his detractors, were offended by Cooper's quiet treatment. Supported by Whig newspapers, already hostile to Cooper, they attacked the *History of the Navy* in reviews so scurrilous and libelous that Cooper later sued and obtained judgments against two of the editors involved, William Stone and Park Benjamin. When Stone's reviewer—William Duer, President of Columbia University!—still insisted that the *History* was inaccurate and unfair, Cooper agreed to submit to a

jury of three lawyers the question of the relative impartiality of
Cooper as a historian and Duer as a reviewer. The decision went
to Cooper.

Within ten years three editions of the complete text of the *History of the Navy* were published as well as three printings of an
abridged version, and translations into German and French were
made almost immediately. Following up the success of this great
work, Cooper did ten brief biographies of naval heroes for *Graham's Magazine,* nine of which were collected in 1846 for a volume entitled *Lives of Distinguished American Naval Officers.* It
is doubtful that any civilian did more in the last century for the
Navy than did this former midshipman.

5

⤳ YIELDING PLACE TO THE NEW

I N 1833 the author returned to Cooperstown after seven years
in Europe. He had, in a sense, been abroad too long, not that
he had acquired aristocratic notions, as some of his critics al-
leged, but rather that he had gotten out of step with the pace of
American life. Unknowingly, he had left the United States at a
moment of great change in the political and social attitudes of the
American people, and when he returned with his own convictions
unchanged, he felt like an alien in his native land. He was still,
as he had always been, a confirmed Jeffersonian, but by now the
country had moved into that later phase of equalitarianism known
as "Jacksonian Democracy." With quixotic zeal Cooper defended
the old order for the last eighteen years of his life in a courageous
but at times wrongheaded stand that did nothing to recapture for
him any of his former favor with the American public.

He understandably became embittered upon his return in 1833
and immediately retreated from New York City to his estate in
Cooperstown. While in Europe he had written five books cham-
pioning the democratic way of life as he knew it; now that way
of life in his own country had changed, and he found himself rejected as a national spokesman. Besides *Notions of the Americans*
and *Letter to General Lafayette,* Cooper had written three his-

torico-political novels, *The Bravo* (1831), *The Heidenmauer* (1832), and *The Headsman* (1833). Each, in its own way, had dealt with the evolution of democratic thought in Europe, *The Bravo* contrasting nominal democracy of the Venetian Republic with real democracy; *The Heidenmauer,* set in Reformation times, picturing the overthrow of a theocratic state by secular forces; and *The Headsman* dramatizing the gross injustices perpetrated in the name of hereditary social rank. But each had also, directly or indirectly, held up the American pattern of democratic government as the ideal in which the rights of the individual were natural, not conceded. In *The Bravo* Cooper had stated:

> A history of the progress of political liberty, written purely in the interests of humanity, is still a desideratum in literature. In nations which have made a false commencement, it would be found that the citizen . . . has extorted immunity after immunity, as his growing intelligence and importance have both instructed and required him to defend those particular rights which were necessary to his well-being. . . . It is scarcely necessary to tell the reader that this freedom . . . depends on a principle entirely different from our own. Here the immunities do not proceed from, but they are granted to the government, being, in other words, concessions of natural rights made by the people to the state for the benefits of social protection. . . . A government which is not properly based on the people possesses an unavoidable and oppressive evil of the first magnitude in the necessity of supporting itself, by physical force and onerous impositions, against the natural action of the majority.

After his return Cooper began to have some second thoughts about "the natural action of the majority," and after nearly five years of silence he enunciated these sober reflections in twelve of the books he wrote between that time and his death in 1851. They first appeared in two forms, as political philosophy in *The American Democrat* (1838), and as fiction in the two-volume sequence *Homeward Bound* (1838) and *Home as Found* (1838). *The American Democrat,* reprinted twice within the twentieth century, is, Cooper declared in the introduction, "written more in the spirit of censure than of praise, for its aim is correction." It is an indictment of the leveling tendency of the 1830's which was, he feared, reducing American culture to its lowest common denominators. Equality, Cooper believed, should apply only to political and civil rights, not to social relationships, and he felt that class distinctions, based on property and education, are inevitable:

> All that democracy means is as equal a participation in rights as is practicable; and to pretend that social equality is a condition of popular institutions is to assume that the latter are destructive of civilization, for, as nothing is more self-evident than the impossibility of raising all men to the highest standard of taste and refinement, the alternative would be to reduce the entire community to the lowest.

The true democrat, he thought, is he who, in the face of any opposition, maintains what he considers to be the highest levels of thought and behavior.

> There is no more capital though more common error than to suppose him an aristocrat who maintains his independence of habits. . . .
> He is the purest democrat who best maintains his rights, and no rights can be dearer to a man of cultivation than exemptions from unseasonable invasions on his time by the coarse minded and ignorant.

Abstract in nature and calm in its plodding analysis of Cooper's political position, *The American Democrat* stirred but little controversy among its readers in 1838. Such was not the case with its fictional counterparts in *Homeward Bound* and *Home as Found*. The first of these, a nautical tale filled with good seamanship and melodrama, brings home from Europe to Templeton the Effingham family, descendants of Judge Temple. It becomes apparent at once that the Effinghams represent the Coopers; Templeton, founded by Judge Temple in *The Pioneers,* had early been identified as Cooperstown founded by Judge William Cooper. During interludes in the voyage the genteel Jeffersonian Effinghams discuss current social and political attitudes with Steadfast Dodge, an "other-directed," equalitarian newspaper editor from the masses of Jacksonian democracy. (Cooper was later to call his type the exponent not of democracy but of mobocracy.) Their talk is quite general compared with the topical allusions of its sequel.

Home as Found uses for part of its plot the perhaps most publicized battle of Cooper's entire life, the Three-Mile Point Controversy. Three miles north of Cooperstown a beautiful wooded cape projects from the west shore of Otsego Lake. It was a place long used for outings by the villagers, and during Cooper's twelve years' absence from Cooperstown there had grown up the mistaken but undisputed belief that the Point was public property left to the people in the will of Judge Cooper. The son's attempts to correct this notion when he returned were suspect: were not these the designs of an aristocrat, lately in Europe, to usurp the property of free Americans? When a tree on the Point was cut and a bathhouse was rebuilt without his being consulted, Cooper placed a notice in the local paper, *The Freeman's Journal,* stating that the Point was private property and that any work done on it required his permission. He was perfectly willing to have his neighbors use the site if they did not abuse it.

> The public is warned against trespassing on the Three Mile Point, it being the intention of the subscriber rigidly to enforce the title of the estate of which he is the representative, to the same. The public has not, nor has ever had, any right to the same, beyond what has been conceded by the liberality of the owners.
>
> J. Fenimore Cooper
> *Executor for the estate of the late Wm. Cooper*

The villagers, many of them transients on the way west, were roused by petty demagogues to organize a mass meeting at which they vowed to disregard Cooper's notice, and voted to request the Franklin Library in Cooperstown to remove from its shelves all of the books written by him. It was a big fuss over nothing; the land was Cooper's and the public had no more rights on it than those he willingly extended. But before he could set forth these simple facts in an open letter—so hot had the issue become that he had to *buy* space in *The Freeman's Journal*—it became a *cause célèbre* picked up by several Whig newspapers, and the version that appeared in Thurlow Weed's influential *Albany Evening Journal* provided reprint copy for the entire American press. Cooper eventually brought suit against two of the New York State editors, but he did not press the case once it was clear that he was in the right and that the editors had misrepresented the case. He was not interested in any settlement for damages, feeling, at this point, that their public embarrassment had taught the journalists a lesson. It was this bruhaha, then known as an "excitement," that Cooper barely disguised in *Home as Found* as the Fishing Point incident. In fact as in fiction, it was the *right* of the individual for which Cooper pleaded as opposed to the *sentiment* of the mass.

❦

The response by journalists to the Effingham novels was immediate and vituperative. James Watson Webb of the *Morning Courier and New York Enquirer* accused Cooper of belittling the institutions of his own country to please European readers; he was, wrote Webb, "a traitor to national pride and national character," and he implored that "the viper so long nourished in our bosoms may shortly leave our shores, never again to disgrace with his presence a land to which he has proved to be an ingrate." This calumny was reprinted by newspapers throughout the country, many of which added jibes of their own. Belatedly it became clear to Cooper that he had been naive in thinking he could shame his critics into silence with the truth; apparently they understood only force, and so he resorted, reluctantly, to punitive measures. When he took legal action against several editors, the replies of the defendants and their journalistic sympathizers were in themselves libelous, precipitating a second round of cases, most of them civil suits for personal damages. Principle left Cooper no room for discretion, and he accepted the challenge of the American press, involved himself in dozens of lawsuits, and spent the rest of his life in almost continuous litigation, serving most of the time as his own counsel. James Watson Webb, William Stone, Park Benjamin, Thurlow Weed, and Horace Greeley were only the most notable of the editors against whom Cooper won court decisions. Some appreciation of the many-leveled libel-lawsuit-libel progression can be gained from the fact that Cooper brought six actions against Thurlow Weed alone in 1841–1842, obtaining five verdicts against the Whig leader.

Whether or not Cooper's courageous and determined stand against the press influenced significantly the future libel laws of New York State is a moot point; what it clearly did accomplish was a sharp curtailment of printed defamations of Cooper's character. He won such a high proportion of his cases that editors finally learned to be cautious. His victories, however, were more satisfying morally than materially, for if the law and the presiding judges were usually on his side, the juries usually were not. They awarded him minimal amounts in the civil suits for damages. After months of delaying tactics by Weed's attorneys in 1841, for example, a jury at Fonda, New York, brought in a verdict for $400—hardly enough to offset Cooper's transportation and personal expenses during that time. But he lost even more financially in the decreased sales of his books. Chastened editors could still retaliate with unfavorable reviews or, worse yet, no reviews at all, and both these devices were used.

To a certain extent, Cooper's troubles with the press were at once both the cause and the effect of the political philosophy of his later years. The rights of the individual, a constant preoccupation with him, seemed too often to be trespassed upon by society through the agency of its newspapers. As he observed time and again, the individual was severely censured, and thus punished, for criticizing society as a whole, while the spokesman for society, the newspaper editor, could ridicule and vilify the individual with impunity. The perfect demonstration of this injustice was his own long ordeal following the publication of his satirical *Home as Found*.

Eventually Cooper came to feel that however necessary the press was for the establishment of a democracy, it might well become detrimental to the continuation of a democratic state. Where the ultimate source of power resides in the people, there also lies the potential for tyranny, and the press, acting as the voice of the people, could become the chief instrument of the great tyrant The Public. Cooper wrote in *The American Democrat:*

> In America it is indispensable that every well wisher of true liberty . . . understand that acts of tyranny can only proceed from the publick. The publick, then, is to be watched in this country, as, in other countries, kings and aristocrats are to be watched.

He felt that being the purveyors and often the creators of public opinion, the newspaper editors are, as a group, to be distrusted. Individuals among them, such as his lifelong friend William Cullen Bryant, he admired, but the type itself he long suspected and finally caricatured in the unpleasant figure of Steadfast Dodge in *Homeward Bound* and *Home as Found*. Snoopy, prying, gossipy, insinuating, Dodge has respect only for public opinion which, unconsciously, he himself helps to determine. Before he makes a decision on any issue, large or small, he takes a poll of popular sentiment on the subject, for he interprets literally the ironic proverb Cooper uses so often, *Vox populi, vox dei* (The voice of the people, the voice of God). And those whom he both fears and attacks are the individuals not so intimidated by the group. He is recognized as the antagonist early in *Homeward Bound* when he announces that he feels it "excessively presuming in an American to pretend to be different from his fellow-citizens."

❧ ❦

Cooper's own difference from most of his fellow citizens of upstate New York reached a climax in the mid-1840's during the land troubles known as the Anti-Rent Wars. From the time of the first white settlements in the state, extensive tracts of land on both sides of the Hudson River, many miles deep in some areas, had been owned by large landholders, the "patroons." The land was worked by tenant farmers to whom leases had been given by the original patroons; in some cases these were for a term of two or three generations, but in the case of the Van Rensselaer holdings the leases were given in perpetuity. The landlords usually retained mining, milling, and lumbering rights for themselves. This was a semifeudal arrangement to which the original tenants voiced little objection when it was a condition of their passage to the New World in the seventeenth century. But gradually it became more and more obnoxious to the descendants of those tenants, and by the nineteenth century they began to rebel against it. Had not their families been on the scene as long as had those of the titleholders? Although the law said otherwise, they felt they had as much right to the land as did the heirs of the patroons. Somehow it was not democratic, they thought, to be required to go on paying rent forever on this land. There were often petty problems that aggravated their dissatisfaction, too, chief among which was the requirement that their rent be paid not outright in cash but "in kind" and in labor. The Van Rensselaer leases usually called for payment of ten to fourteen bushels of wheat plus four fat hens and the labor of the tenant and his team for a period of from one to five days per year.

Coupled with the reluctance of the tenants to pay their rent was, in many instances, their inability to do so. The thin soil of New York State, soon exhausted by too intensive cultivation, was unable to yield enough to compete with the newly opened Midwestern lands, and many of the tenants fell into debt. During the 1830's back rents on the Van Rensselaer holdings alone mounted to over $400,000, an enormous sum in those days. It was widely rumored that Stephen ("The Good Patroon") Van Rensselaer would in his will cancel these debts, but when that document was probated after his death in 1839, it was discovered that he had assigned this money outstanding to a trust fund for his heirs; under these circumstances, his two sons, acting as his executors, had no choice but to press for its payment. When the rent was not forthcoming, sheriffs were sent to collect it or evict the tenants. But by now the farmers were organized, and they drove off the less audacious deputies and tarred and feathered the more persistent. Governor Seward sent the militia to the Van Rensselaer lands in the Helderberg Mountains, back of Albany, in 1839 to restore order, and appointed a committee to try to arrange for the sale of the land to willing tenants in exchange for easy, long-term mortgages. But the Van Rensselaers did not really want to sell, and the negotiations soon broke down. As the election of 1844 approached, Seward's successor, William Bouck, considered it inexpedient to antagonize several thousand tenant voters, who were again stirring, to satisfy the legal demands of a few dozen landlords; but he was forced to send three companies of militia to Hudson to prevent anti-renters from storming a jail in order to release their leader, "Big Thunder," Dr. Smith A. Boughton. Barns and haystacks of landlords were burned and crops were trampled down by bands of tenants disguised as Indians in masks and calico. In 1845, the newly elected governor, Silas Wright, proclaimed Delaware County in a state of insurrection after a deputy sheriff had been murdered at an eviction sale, and everywhere there was growing support for the anti-rent movement. Later in 1845 seventeen large landholders, seeing the handwriting on the wall, announced their willingness to sell, and when the legislature convened in Albany in 1846, both parties, eyeing hungrily the large bloc of tenant votes, sought ways of forcing the remaining landlords to relinquish their legal claims to the lands. A law was passed making more difficult the repossession of acreages for rent delinquency; another imposed a special tax on rent from long-term leases, a special discriminatory income tax. Po-litically, it was a conflict between popular will and existing law; morally, the forces in conflict were expediency and principle.

Cooper, interested not at all in the politics involved but in the morality, entered the fray in 1845 with the first two volumes of a trilogy in support of the position of the landlords. None of the Cooper land was affected, as his father had not dealt in long-term leases, so he had nothing to gain personally; and from the point of view of book sales, he had much to lose by antagonizing thousands of tenants and hundreds of thousands of their sympathizers. But when had Cooper ever forsaken principle for expedient silence? He published *Satanstoe* and *The Chainbearer* in 1845 and in the following year a concluding volume, *The Redskins*, all three of them supposedly taken from the "Littlepage Manuscripts."

The trilogy is a genealogical work tracing the fortunes of the Littlepage family from the days of the French and Indian War when they open up a settlement on the New York State frontier until the troubled 1840's when their holdings are placed in jeop-ardy by mobs of anti-rent rioters. The Littlepage story is a care-fully detailed fictional version of what Cooper saw as the history of the typical landholding family in the state. Each volume is a first-person narrative related by a Littlepage descendant who, in his turn, is about to inherit the family estates and assume the re-sponsibility for their operation. Cooper's handling of the narrative method here illustrates well the developing competence of his craftsmanship in these later years. By having as his autobiograph-ical observer a Littlepage, Cooper allowed the landlord group to present its own story in the most favorable and human light. And in each volume the narrator is a *young* Littlepage who enters the deep forest, rescues a fair maiden from some impending danger, and eventually marries her. What reader could resist such fairy-tale appeal for his sympathy?

◅ ▻

Of the three books, the first, in the judgment of most critics, is by far the best. This may be attributed in part to the fact that *Satanstoe* is the least patently propagandistic of the novels, being farthest removed in time from the incidents of the 1840's which provoked the trilogy. Like *The Pioneers*, it is a sociological study of the late eighteenth-century frontier in upstate New York, showing the interaction of different groups in the new lands and giving the reader accurate vignettes of the customs and manners of the day. Cornelius Littlepage, the narrator, inspects the family tract at Mooseridge, north of Albany, fights Indians in the bush and the French at Ticonderoga (as part of Abercromby's ill-fated expedition in 1758), courts and marries Anneke Mordaunt, heiress to an adjacent estate called Ravensnest, and at the end settles down as the great landlord of his generation. He undertakes to have the forests cleared, improvements made, and tenant farmers settled on his holdings, all at great expense to himself—so great, he assures the reader, that it will require generations of tenants' rent to enable the Littlepages to recapture their investment. Only one of Littlepage's prospective tenants, a Connecticut Yankee named Jason Newcome, offers any objection to the leases extended, and Jason finds little support, at this stage, among his fellows. It is he, however, who is the antagonist, and as the trilogy progresses, it will be the Newcomes who will agitate effectively for a cessation of all payments of rent. But here, under the old agrarian order that Cooper loved, demagoguery made little headway.

Satanstoe is a gay and colorful work despite its being a problem novel. "Corny," the young hero, travels from the family seat, Satanstoe, in Westchester County, to New York City, sees the wonders of the metropolis and its social life, including a production of Addison's *Cato,* and observes a Pinkster Festival, the annual saturnalia of the slaves. Before forsaking civilization for the overland trek to Mooseridge and Ravensnest, Corny spends another holiday farther north in Albany, enjoying several of the popular pastimes of that era. With his Dutch friend Guert Ten Eyck, his fiancée Anneke Mordaunt, and a party of young people he skates on the frozen Hudson River, coasts down State Street hill, visits a noted fortuneteller, and steals the mayor's dinner in a prank typical of the robust humor of eighteenth-century New Yorkers. Laughter and high spirits prevail, and it is not until the next volume, *The Chainbearer,* that Cooper begins to suggest the extent and gravity of the social change he is chronicling.

ఆ§ §ఌ

Corny's son, Mordaunt, is the narrator of the second novel, *The Chainbearer*. By this time, just after the American Revolution, the relationship between landlord and tenant has begun to change, and he is continually forced to underplay his role in order to maintain a semblance of equality. He marries not a landed heiress, as his father had, but the niece of a surveyor. Even his largesse is restricted; he is warned that inviting all his tenants to an old-fashioned landlord's dinner would now offend many of them. The family still deals in long-term leases and in the course of the book he issues a number of them "for three lives . . . no one objecting to the rent, which, it was admitted all round, was not only reasonable but low." There is a growing undercurrent of unrest, however, that is to become overt in the final volume, *The Redskins*, but as yet the objection is confined to innuendo, oblique resistance, and the untenable lawlessness of squatters.

When his two designated heirs die prematurely, Jason Newcome, claiming that his rights have been abused, haggles about the terms of his three-lives lease. Mordaunt generously renews for another three lives the lease to Jason's farm after pointing out— as Cooper had to his neighbors during the Three-Mile Point Controversy—that the *right* to land is a matter of legal commitment, not feelings. The issue of the Newcome lease occasions a brief discussion about property rights that serves as a prelude to the full-scale debate on the question that takes place in the lumber camp of Aaron Thousandacres, a squatter who has been cutting and milling a section of the Littlepage forest. Who really owns the land, the man with a claim to having inherited it from his ancestors or the one who possesses it and whose industry makes it produce? The argument that the original white settlers used against the Indians is now being turned against them by enterprising newcomers, an irony fully appreciated by Susquesus, the wise old Onondaga friend of the Littlepages who appears in all three volumes. The question of ownership Mordaunt would have dismissed quickly and referred to his lawyers had he not been captured by Thousandacres and his troop of rustic, rawboned sons, who detain him at their camp until they can dispose of their illegally gained stockpile of prime lumber. Held captive, he has no choice but to hear, and he is drawn into a lengthy forum, continuing over several chapters, on property ownership and property rights; the debate serves as a sounding board for different points of view: that of the landlord, that of the satisfied tenant, that of the dissatisfied tenant, that of the squatter who takes the law into his own hands, and that of the Indian.

Less articulate than any of the disputants but symbolic of law and order is the Littlepage surveyor, old Andries Coejmans, a descendant of the first white settlers in the area, the Dutch; he is "the chainbearer," and the measuring links he carries throughout the novel suggest not only legal ownership of land but the restrictions of law within which people must live in an orderly society. Andries' personal conflict with both the scheming Yankee, Newcome, and the lawless Thousandacres, who eventually kills him in a scuffle, provides an allegorically dramatic parallel to the abstract debate at Aaron's camp. Susquesus avenges the death of the chainbearer by shooting Thousandacres, but it is not very reassuring to have one wrong cancel out another, and the reader is left with the uncomfortable feeling that beneath the tranquillity finally restored to the settlement lies a growing discontent that may erupt again at any time.

ം§ ൧ം

A generation is skipped between *The Chainbearer* and *The Redskins,* the narrator of the last volume being Hugh, the grandson of Mordaunt Littlepage. If Cooper originally intended a continuous history of New York State to his own times, he may have been forced to relinquish that design by the rapidly worsening position of the landlords during 1845. Unless he could bring his guns to bear on the aggressive anti-rent forces before they had won the war, his whole effort would be futile. It is in deference to the persuasive purpose of the series, then, that its artistic pattern is violated as Cooper leaps ahead more than fifty years in the Littlepage chronicle. His haste to rush this concluding volume into print is reflected in its poor plotting and its failure to integrate theme with character and action. It is, in other words, too obviously propagandistic to be satisfying as literature.

An absentee landlord enjoying the tourist sights of Europe, Hugh comes back to an America that is different from his expectations. His failure to sympathize with its equalitarian thrust is reminiscent of Cooper's own attitude when he returned from abroad, except that Hugh's dilemma lies in the real world instead of in the realm of theory; his livelihood depends upon the *status quo*. Hugh arrives home just after an uprising of his tenants, encouraged indirectly by a government tolerant to their demands for land reform. So powerful are the anti-rent partisans that Hugh and Uncle Ro, his adviser and traveling companion, fearing for their lives, travel to Ravensnest in disguise, though, ironically, they hear an agitator picture Hugh as a powerful aristocrat against whom the tenants are locked in mortal combat. This is but one of the rationalizations by which the tenants try to persuade themselves and the world at large that theirs is a just cause. Unable to find any flaw in their leases, they shift to an *ad hominem* approach, attacking the real and imagined offenses of the Littlepages. They *imagine* Hugh to be despotic and vengeful, basing their inference upon his personal differences from the crowd. The canopied pew that the Littlepage family has always had in the local church becomes for them not just an anachronism now but a symbol of class distinction, as do all the Littlepage accoutrements down to their very tableware, as a demagogue reveals while vilifying Hugh before a gathering of tenants:

"He is no man for a pewter spoon and two-pronged fork! No, my countrymen! He must have a *gold* spoon for some of his dishes, and you will find it hard to believe—plain, unpretending republican farmers that you are, but it is not the less true—he must have forks of *silver!* Fellow-citizens, Hugh Littlepage would not put his knife into his mouth, as you and I do in eating—as all plain, unpretending republicans do—for all the world. It would choke him; no, he keeps *silver* forks to touch his anointed lips!"

The subtitle, *Indian and Injin*, is a reference to the contrast Cooper tries to develop between real red men and the marauding tenants disguised as Indians. He has a group of Plains Indians en route to Washington make a wide detour to Ravensnest to pay their respects to the now venerable Susquesus, and while they are there they break up an attack on the manor house made by their false counterparts. For what it contributes, too much time and space are expended on this maneuver. The transparent disguise of the anti-renters is really a trivial detail on which to pivot so much action, and the failure in artistic proportion here is symptomatic of Cooper's loss of objectivity in the later stages of the contest. Like Hugh, his protagonist at bay, Cooper strikes out in all directions, and the tone of *The Redskins* is sharper than that of most of his novels.

The reader is not unprepared for this stridency if he has first examined the preface of the book. There Cooper condemns in the

Otsego Hall.
Built by William C Cooper in 1798, the home of James Fenimore Cooper
from 1834 to 1851, destroyed by fire in 1853.

WATERCOLOR, PHOTOGRAPH FROM THE NEW YORK STATE HISTORICAL ASSOCIATION, COOPERSTOWN

strongest terms the tendency to permit popular sentiment to repu-
diate contractual commitments: ". . . this is not liberty, but tyranny in its worst form." All of his misgivings about the direction
taken by American democracy in these later years of his life
come to a focus on the role of government in the anti-rent conflict:

> The state is bound to make all classes of men respect its laws, and
> in nothing more so than in the fulfillment of their legal contracts.
> The greater the number of the offenders, the higher the obligation
> to act with decision and efficiency. To say that these disorganizers
> *ought* not to be put down is to say that crime is to obtain impunity
> by its own extent; and to say that they *cannot* be put down
> "under our form of government" is a direct admission that the gov-
> ernment is unequal to the discharge of one of the plainest and
> commonest obligations of all civilized society. If this be so, the
> sooner we get rid of the present form of government, the better.

At the close of *The Redskins* the issue between landowner and
tenant, law and sentiment, is still unresolved, with the tenants in
actual control of the Littlepage lands and Hugh in retreat to
Washington to engage in last-ditch litigation. How much time the
legal proceedings brought by the landlords would require neither
Hugh nor Cooper could know. They took, in fact, many years,
and though all the decisions but one upheld the validity of the
leases, the tenants had won a Fabian victory. By then the landlords, under duress, had sold off their acreages, the last of the Van
Rensselaer holdings being purchased by two speculators in 1850,
and their most voluble spokesman, James Fenimore Cooper, had
died.

Although he wrote five novels after the publication of the anti-
rent trilogy, including two of his most successful sea tales, *Jack
Tier* and *The Sea Lions,* Cooper's best bolts of criticism had been
expended. Of his two later socio-political works only *The Crater*
(1847) has received the attention of modern readers. A story
that, on the surface, appears to be a South Sea idyl, it is actually
a political and social allegory in which Cooper recapitulates the
whole history of the United States. Two survivors of a shipwreck,
Mark Woolston, first mate, and Bob Betts, able-bodied seaman,
wash ashore on a recently formed volcanic island which they possess as their own Garden of Eden. After adventures akin to those

of Robinson Crusoe, with some literal indebtedness to Defoe, they bring a group of settlers to the island, including the Woolston family, and Mark becomes the governor of this new country. Aided only by a council, Mark expects to rule the island for life in order "to prevent the . . . corrupting influence of politics, viz., election from getting too much sway over the public mind."

All goes well at first in this Pacific paradise, but the inevitable serpents make their appearance in the forms of a journalist-printer, a lawyer, and four evangelical Protestant clergymen, a Baptist, a Methodist, a Presbyterian, and a Quaker. They arrive with a second group of immigrants, secretly recruited by some of the original settlers who have grown dissatisfied with Mark's conservative Episcopal minister, Mr. Hornblower. The competing denominations encourage factional antipathies, the lawyer promotes business by instructing the people on the values of litigation, and the printer starts a rabble-rousing newspaper, *The Crater Truth-Teller*. A clique of demagogues gains popular support to change the whole complexion of life in Mark's little Utopia. The constitution is altered (as in actuality the New York State Constitution was modified in 1846) to make all offices elective, and so Mark is deposed as governor when his prescribed term expires; after he retires to private life, they start legal proceedings against his title to that part of the crater he had retained as his own. In this microcosm of America the parallel between events on the island and those in New York during the 1840's is at once obvious. As the book is a fantasy, however, an island that springs miraculously from the ocean floor can just as miraculously recede again into the depths; this is what happens to the crater when its paradise is totally lost to the forces of evil. Mark and his family leave the island in disgust, and when they return a few months later, find no trace of it above the surface of the sea. This striking climax has been called a *deus ex machina* and a puerile piece of wish fulfillment on Cooper's part, defeating in fiction those forces which in the real world were impervious to his attacks. It is probably neither of these but rather Cooper's loudest jeremiad on the worsening state of affairs in America. Springing up in the Western Hemisphere with the blessing of the Lord, might not the American republic, deteriorating morally, fall from grace and know the fate of Sodom and Gomorrah? It was a prophetic warning of the destruction Cooper saw ahead if men did not soon reform.

6

❧ YANKEES AND YORKERS

I N THE criticism of America for which the novels of Cooper's
later life often served as vehicles, it is possible to see the mythmaker at work again. Just as he had made articulate the collective
beliefs about and attitudes toward the great American wilderness
and had identified its folk heroes, so too he developed from the
political and social movements of his day a legendary world with
its own *dramatis personae.* From the abstract realm in which it so
largely existed, he projected the conflict between the values of
Jeffersonian democracy and those of Jacksonian democracy into
the history of New York State's relations with its neighbors to
the east. Sir Walter Scott had found material for romance in the
centuries-old border warfare between England and Scotland; his
American counterpart exploited for fictional purposes the long-
standing hostility between New Yorkers and Yankees. Cooper dif-
fered sharply from his predecessor, however, in his auctorial commitment. If Scott could as often write from the English point of
view, regardless of his personal sympathies, as he did from the
Scottish, Cooper could not be as ostensibly nonpartisan. His sympathies remained consistently on the west side of the Berkshire
Mountains.

❧ ❈

Cooper's antipathy to New Englanders was only his personal expression of the larger cultural clash of Yankees and New Yorkers. Between New York and her neighbors to the east there had always been friction. On the shores of the Connecticut River in the 1630's the original Dutchmen of New Netherlands and the first Puritans of New England had eyed each other with mutual suspicion, and the seeds of bad feeling then sown had borne bitter fruit for two centuries. There was a constant state of border warfare, usually a cold war fought in social and economic terms, though on occasions there were actual hostilities. But the course of empire irrevocably took its westward way, New Englanders could not be confined forever to their acres of flint, and New York during the eighteenth century was overrun by emigrants from the east. Twelve hundred sleigh loads of them passed through Albany during one three-day period in 1795. Lured by the advertisements, often fraudulent, of land companies, and inflamed by the "Genesee Fever," Yankees poured across the border.

Many of them, members of either the Connecticut or Ohio land companies, having the great Western Reserve as their destination, used New York State simply as a stopping place, and as a result earned for their group a reputation for restlessness and wanderlust. Like Tennyson's Ulysses, they had "become a name . . . For always roaming. . . ." A deeply rooted New Yorker and one of Cooper's most lovable folk characters, "the commodore," points this up in a good-humored conversation with a companion in *Home as Found*. The Yankees, he says,

> "are the worst neighbors that a man can have. . . . I often go away of a morning to pass the day on the water, and, on returning home at night, find half the houses filled with new faces."
>
> "Well, well, my good friend, take consolation. You'll meet all the faces you ever saw here, one day, in heaven."
>
> "Never! Not a man of them will stay there, if there be such a thing as moving. Depend on it, sir," added the commodore, in the simplicity of his heart, "heaven is no place for a Yankee, if he can get further west by hook or by crook. They are all too uneasy for any steady occupation."

Others lingered in the rich river bottoms and were largely responsible for the rapid settlement and development of central and western New York after the Revolution. They were, to be sure, welcomed by certain interests in the state: the businessmen, the landholding companies, and such conquerors of the wilderness as William Cooper. The old Judge, in fact, held them in great respect:

> As to those western counties of New York, which I have been describing, they are chiefly peopled from the New England states, where the people are civil, well-informed, and very sagacious. So that a wise stranger would be much apter to conform at once to their usages than to begin by teaching them better.

But by other established families—such as the Van Rensselaers, the DeLanceys, the Schuylers—the Yankees were often bitterly resented, and socially it was with this York State landed gentry, rather than with his enterprising father, that Cooper was sympathetic.

The Yankee was not only a native of New England. He was also an American folk hero of the nineteenth century, and it is not surprising that he should be included in the character gallery of a writer as alert to the oral tradition as Cooper was. What is of interest, however, is the way in which he slowly evolved in Cooper's books over the years from a folk type to a full-fledged symbol of social evil. The process is revealing of Cooper's methods as a receiver and shaper of the American heritage.

The down-Easter was a protean figure, appearing in various yarns now as a bumpkin, greenhorn, or comic rustic, awkward in his movement, twangy in his speech (Yankee Doodle or Brother Jonathan); now as a "natural man" endowed with peasant shrewdness and a stock of horse sense (Lowell's Hosea Biglow); now as adventurer, tall talker, and himself the subject of tall talk (Sam Patch and Major Jack Downing); now as a homespun philosopher and cracker-barrel wit (Sam Slick); and again as slicker, trickster, sharper, and general American cony-catcher. His roles were legion, his plastic personality responding to the diverse demands of time, place, and circumstance. He appeared to different people in different guises, and sometimes in various forms to the same observer. Cooper saw him at first as partly comic, but as the novelist shifted his gaze away from the American scene, the puck turned demon, and whenever Cooper looked at him after 1833, he saw only the grim goblin features.

Yankees in Cooper's early works follow the standard variations on the type. In *The Spy* Cooper refers to his Yankee, Harvey Birch, simply as "a native of one of the eastern colonies." Harvey, when the reader first meets him, is a peddler who channels into the art of espionage the near-necromancy of his trade. If, in the novel, he does not charm into his pockets the gold and silver of the community, in the fashion of Yankee traders described so colorfully by Constance Rourke in *American Humor,* it is not because his powers have failed him. He has already had a successful career as itinerant merchant, Cooper affirms a number of times, and the hoard of gold which he has amassed plays a conspicuously integral part in the plot. The reader is permitted on one occasion to witness Harvey's almost ritual display of the wonders of his pack and to view the predictably hypnotic effect which it has on the young ladies of his audience:

> Sarah gave but little time for the usual salutations before she commenced her survey of the contents of the pack; and, for several minutes, the two were engaged in bringing to light the various articles it contained. The tables, chairs, and floor were soon covered with silks, crapes, gloves, muslins, and all the stock of an itinerant trader. . . .
>
> The peddler, burying his body in the pack, brought forth a quantity of lace of exquisite fineness, and, holding it up to view, he required the admiration of the young lady. Miss Peyton dropped the cup she was engaged in washing from her hand; and Frances exhibited the whole of that lovely face. . . .
>
> The aunt quitted her employment; and soon Birch disposed of a large portion of this valuable article.

But for the time being, at least, Harvey's trade has been forsaken, except as it serves to disguise his new endeavor, spying for the American forces, and whatever onus was attached to his former business practices is absolved, in the mind of the reader, by the generosity of his patriotic sentiments. But the skills of the peddler are very much in evidence throughout the book, and the adroitness of his secret maneuvers about the Neutral Ground of Westchester County exploits to the utmost all the shrewdness, ingenuity, and insight into human nature so frequently associated with the Yankee type.

Perhaps the most truly comic Yankee in Cooper's collection of down-Easters is David Gamut, the psalmodist of *The Last of the*

Mohicans. His description alone would identify him as a stage Yankee:

> The person of this individual was to the last degree ungainly without being in any particular manner deformed. He had all the bones and joints of other men, without any of their proportions. Erect, his stature surpassed that of his fellows; seated, he appeared reduced within the ordinary limits of the race. The same contrariety in his members seemed to exist throughout the whole man. His head was large; his shoulders narrow; his arms long and dangling; while his hands were small. . . . His legs and thighs were thin . . . but of extraordinary length; and his knees would have been considered tremendous, had they not been outdone by the broader foundations on which this false superstructure of the blended human orders was so profanely reared. The ill-assorted and injudicious attire of the individual only served to render his awkwardness more conspicuous. A sky-blue coat, with short and broad skirts and low cape, exposed a long thin neck, and longer and thinner legs. . . . His nether garment was of yellow nankeen, closely fitted to the shape, and tied at his bunches of knees by large knots of white riband, a good deal sullied by use. . . . A large, civil cocked hat, like those worn by clergymen within the last thirty years, surmounted the whole, furnishing dignity to a good-natured and somewhat vacant countenance, that apparently needed such artificial aid, to support the gravity of some high and extraordinary trust.

With but slight alteration, here is a reconstructed Ichabod Crane, Irving's psalm-singing Yankee schoolmaster of Sleepy Hollow.

David's veneration for the Hebrew psalms is obsessive, and therein lies his comedy. The well-tuned psalm is to him the panacea for all the ills of the world, and he marches zealously through the novel armed with pitchpipe and psaltery, singing to any willing audience of frontier passersby—soldiers, settlers, Indians, or even the wild beasts of the forest. In his most ludicrous moment in the tale, he is surprised in the act of trying to teach sacred song to a pack of beavers, reputedly wise animals. To Natty Bumppo, ordinarily rather saturnine but now convulsed in paroxysms of silent laughter, he reasons, "It would seem that the Being that gave them power to improve his gifts so well would not deny them voices to proclaim his praise." After this episode, the reader is no longer tempted to take him seriously as a singing John the Baptist in the great American wilderness nor to mistake the comedy for pathos.

⋘ ⋙

The Yankee was bad enough in his native habitat; he was worse out of it. Among the yeomen in the comfortable New Yorker squirearchy he was a disquieting influence. He demanded equal status with the landlord; he did not know his place; he showed no respect for his betters; he was a social leveler—these were among the things that the gentry said of him. Through the narrator in *Satanstoe,* Cooper remarks:

> "There is, and can be no greater absurdity than to imagine that the sheer neighborhood, or proximity of position, makes men acquainted. That was one of Jason Newcome's *Connecticut* notions. Having been educated in a state of society in which all associated on a certain footing of intimacy, and in which half the difficulties that occurred were 'told to the church,' he was forever fancying he knew all the gentry of Westchester, because he had lived a year or two in the county; when, in fact, he had never spoken to one in a dozen of them."

Joel Strides, the villain of *Wyandotté,* shares this equalitarian bias:

> It was distasteful to Joel Strides . . . to see a social chasm as wide as that which actually existed between the family of the proprietor of the Knoll and his own growing no narrower. . . . Utterly incapable of appreciating the width of that void which separates the gentleman from the man of coarse feelings and illiterate vulgarity, he began to preach that doctrine of exaggerated and mistaken equality which says "one man is as good as another," a doctrine that is nowhere engrafted even on the most democratic of our institutions today, since it would totally supersede the elections, and leave us to draw lots for public trusts, as men are drawn for juries.

Despite his pretension to social equality with the Jeffersonian gentlemen, the Yankee was all too obviously a vulgarian. To Cooper he was a symbol of all the defects of American democracy approaching mid-century. He denied all value to that inevitable formation of social classes according to educational achievement which Cooper had championed in *The American Democrat*. He wanted fashion to comply with the taste of the masses; he was an exponent of "mobocracy." All that he was too insensitive to understand or appreciate, he proscribed. Cooper writes of the Yankee:

> Unused to intercourse with what was then called the great world of the provinces, he knew not how to appreciate its manners or opinions; and, as is usual with the provincial, he affected to despise that which he neither practised nor understood. This, at once, indisposed him to acknowledge the distinctions of classes; and, when accident threw him into the adjoining province, he became marked at once for decrying the usages he encountered, comparing them with singular self-felicitation to those he had left behind him; sometimes with justice beyond a doubt, but oftener in provincial ignorance and narrow bigotry.

Coming from the land of the town meeting, the Yankee took democratic processes for granted and was not inhibited by that peasant complex which so long hampered the members of the York State patroon serfdom. He demanded a voice in government and stirred his recalcitrant neighbors to take political action. It is the Yankees Aristabulus Bragg and Steadfast Dodge in *Home as Found* who instigate the townspeople of Templeton to demand as theirs the picknicking area owned by the Effinghams. Later it is Yankee treachery in the persons of Jason Newcome and his heirs which undermines the House of Littlepage and incites rebellion against the completely legal land leases in Cooper's anti-rent trilogy. Statute law often means nothing to Cooper's American aggressor as he sweeps westward. The popular will at the moment constitutes the only law he recognizes, and this he often predetermines through demagoguery and agitation. For him, the majority must rule not only in political matters but in personal affairs too; the Yankee in Cooper is an exponent of that "other directed" society which Riesman was to define a century later. Aristabulus Bragg even suggests that Edward Effingham had been unethical in ignoring the architectural taste of his neighbors when he remodeled his home, "The Wigwam," along Gothic lines:

> "I admire the house, and know it to be a perfect specimen of a pure architecture in its way, but then public opinion is not quite up to it. I see all its beauties . . . but then there are many, a

COOPER IN 1850, OIL BY A. BIGELOW AFTER THE BRADY DAGUERREOTYPE

majority, perhaps, who do not, and these persons think they ought to be consulted about such matters. . . . In a republican government, you undoubtedly understand . . . it will rule all things."

Religiously, the Yankee was determined not to be assimilated and he carried his gods with him over the Berkshires. Alongside the church the meeting house sprang up, and with it "the rowdy religion—half cant, half blasphemy—that Cromwell and his associates entailed on so many Englishmen." With the ritual, the stylized décor, the impersonality, and the church-centeredness of Anglicanism, the Yankee was unsympathetic. His was a highly personalized religion, introspective, soul-searching, often emotional, and rarely objectified in concrete symbols. Concerned not only with the state of his own soul but with the spiritual welfare of the whole community, he threw himself zealously into movements aimed at reform and moral reawakening. Ithuel Bolt, the down-Easter of *The Wing-and-Wing,* " 'experienced religion,' and, at this moment, is an active abolitionist, a patron of the temperance cause, and a general terror to evildoers, under the appellation of Deacon Bolt." Carrying their Jacksonian politics over to their religion, Cooper's Yankees insist on rotation in church office as a healthy stimulant to religious life. Without it zeal and enthusiasm might flag, and there might ensue a religious calm tantamount to spiritual stagnation. In *Home as Found* Yankee-Dissenter Aristabulus Bragg debates clerical rotation with New Yorker-Anglican Eve Effingham:

"Now, Miss Effingham, everyone thinks frequent changes of religious instructors . . . necessary. There can be no vital piety without keeping the flame alive with excitement."

"I confess, sir, that my own reasoning would lead to a directly contrary conclusion, and that there can be no vital piety, as you term it, with excitement."

* * * *

"That may be the case in France, Miss Effingham, but in America we look to excitement as the great purifier. We should as soon expect the air in the bottom of a well to be elastic, as that the moral atmosphere shall be clear and salutary without the breezes of excitement. For my part . . . I think that no man should be a judge in the same court more than ten years at a time, and a priest gets to be rather common-place and flat after five."

Along with these "dissenting" tendencies went the usual "blue law" attitude attributed to the Puritans by their detractors. Dancing, drinking, and gaming of all kinds were clearly pastimes of the damned. In *Satanstoe* Corny Littlepage writes:

> "I felt a disposition to laugh outright at the manner in which Jason betrayed a sneaking consciousness of crime, as he saw my meek . . . and warm-hearted mother lay the cards on the table that evening. . . . [He] had been educated under the narrow and exaggerated notions of a provincial sect, and had obtained a species of conscience that was purely dependent on his miserable schooling."

More and more his satire of the Yankee took on an emotional coloring as Cooper's relationship with the American public began to disintegrate in the 1830's and 1840's. Rejected as a champion of the democratic cause, Cooper had become embittered toward democracy itself, and the feelings of the repulsed suitor were mixed, alternately tender and brutal, at once wounded and wounding. As the web of his tragic fate closed about Cooper, he looked in desperation for an opponent to hold responsible, a foe against whom to vent his rage; and he found the Yankee. Here was the Cooperian white whale, and whether it was evil itself or only the pasteboard puppet of social evil, Cooper burst his hot heart's shell against it, and all as futilely as Ahab was to assault Moby Dick. Yankee-baiting became an obsession with Cooper, and the Yankee came to be a symbol of all that was disturbing in his personal life as well as all that was wrong with life in America. It was virtually a pathological reaction.

The hypocrite, the miser, the false friend, the schemer, the unscrupulous opportunist, the demagogue, the rabid enthusiast are the roles he gives to such Yankees as Steadfast Dodge and Aristabulus Bragg in *Homeward Bound* and *Home as Found*, Joel Strides in *Wyandotté*, Jason and Seneca Newcome in the anti-rent trilogy, and Deacon Pratt in *The Sea Lions*. By now Cooper might have adapted Artemus Ward's anti-Indian maxim and maintained that "Yankees is pizen, wherever found." What other men do with impunity earns for the Yankee only abuse. In *Wyandotté*, for example, both Jamie Allen and Joel Strides are Calvinists and Dissenters, but while Jamie is always an upright lad in his differences from the norm, the Connecticut man is "wily," "jesuitical," "sneering," and "insinuating." Or again, at the end of *Home as Found,* when each of the characters is being accounted for and ushered out of the novel, in the deliberate fashion of much nineteenth-century fiction, Aristabulus Bragg exits westward toward the frontier, there to turn his hand to anything that offers itself, to "practice law, or keep school, or to go to Congress, or to turn trader, or to saw lumber," or, as he eventually does do, "to tend a store in the absence of its owner." Here, except for the schoolteaching, was a list of the very jobs that Abraham Lincoln held during these same decades, labors that lent themselves so readily to the legend of his prairie years. But no glory accrues to Bragg for his ability to adapt to the task at hand, and his energy and enterprise are cheapened with the epithet "goaheadism." If perchance the Yankee already has money, he does not enjoy it or invest it in enterprises that will benefit the community as well as himself, for both the gracious living and the *noblesse oblige* of the Littlepages are unknown to him. He hoards his wealth, practices "the most ruthless extortion" to get more, speculates shrewdly, and dies clutching a bag of ill-gotten gold, as Deacon Ichabod Pratt does in *The Sea Lions.*

Along with the Yankee's major sins were peccadilloes that singled him out as a distinct type. He had an unconscionably ugly dialectal pronunciation of English, which seems to have struck Cooper at times as sheer perverseness. He showed no interest in the traditions cherished in the area into which he moved. Such Dutch customs as Pinkster Festival and the celebrations connected with the annual arrival of St. Nicholas were not carried on by the Yankee or his descendants. Nor did he have any respect for Dutch place names. *Hell-gate* should be bowdlerized to *Hurl-gate* or *Whirl-gate,* he claimed. And the Yankee argues that the fictitious name *Satanstoe,* in the novel of that title, was probably a Dutch corruption of *Devilton* or *Dibbleton.* A New Yorker in that novel complains:

> "Since the eastern troops have begun to come among us, indeed, they have commenced a desperate inroad on many of our venerated Dutch names; names that the English, direct from home, have generally respected. Indeed change—change in all things seems to be the besetting passion of these people."

❧ ❧

There is a dilemma, of course, when the features of both sympathetic and unsympathetic types come along together in the same character, and this happens occasionally when the hated Yankee is also the beloved old salt. Which aspect dominates? The answer usually depends on the year of the character's creation. In the early novels, while Cooper yet felt no disaffection for American life, the Yankee features are hardly noticeable in the dual type. Long Tom Coffin, for example, is as down-East as he can be, a son of the most famous sea-faring family of Nantucket, and yet no one among the Cooperian heroes is more memorably likable, except perhaps Natty Bumppo himself.

Captain Truck, of the *Montauk,* makes his appearance a decade later, in the 1830's, and here the Yankee lineage, though still subdued, is more in evidence for a while. The conflict in Cooper's mind between realism and romance, between satire and exaltation, between negative and positive attitudes toward the contemporary scene are nowhere better exhibited. *Homeward Bound* and *Home as Found* were originally to be all one novel, a novel of satire. When the work commenced, Truck was apparently to be a stereotyped Yankee boor, for in the opening chapters of *Homeward Bound* he is offensive to the Effingham group, the protagonists of the novel. Lacking in gentility, an unwelcome and uncouth intruder on the private conversations of his passengers, he depreciates the one social grace he has by overusing it. He is fascinated with the art of social introductions, and he insists on introducing all hands round whenever a group gathers on deck, even though all its members may already be well acquainted. But the story soon gets out of hand, its satire is postponed, and before Cooper can bring the work under control again, one volume has been filled with preliminary action, the voyage home from England. Cooper remarks:

In one respect, this book is a parallel to Franklin's well-known apologue of the hatter and his sign. *It was commenced with a sole view to exhibit the present state of society in the United States,* through the agency, in part, of a set of characters . . . who had freshly arrived from Europe. . . . By the original plan, the work was to open at the threshold of the country. . . . But a consultation with others has left little more of this plan than the hatter's friends left of his sign. As a vessel was introduced in the first chapter, the cry was for "more ship," until the work has be-

> come "all ship"; it actually closing at, or near, the spot where it
> was originally intended it should commence. Owing to this diversion
> from the author's design . . . a necessity has been created of run-
> ning the tale through two separate works . . . . (Italics mine)

Actually, it is more likely that once afloat, Cooper was simply in-
dulging his passion for the sea.

After a five-hundred-page demonstration of courage and seamanship, Truck can hardly turn out to be a villain. He under-
stands the code of heroes and acts according to its dictates; if he
is still somewhat graceless socially, he exhibits grace under pres-
sure. Truck earns the respect of the author, the reader, and the
other characters, and when the *Montauk* docks in New York, he
accepts the invitation of the Effinghams to visit them at their
Templeton estate. Once there, he is joshed about his Connecticut
origins, but he is clearly a species apart from Steadfast Dodge
and Aristabulus Bragg and their Yankee followers.

By the 1840's Cooper's animosity toward New England character had become so inveterate that he was incapable of letting
even sea-faring Yankees go by in peace. Ithuel Bolt in *The Wing-
and-Wing* (1842) is not only a seaman but a badly mistreated
one, having suffered impressment by the British navy. He has,
thus, a double claim on the reader's sympathy, but it is given
only grudgingly, for Bolt is shown to be as sly and mean and de-
ceitful as Joel Strides and Jason Newcome. If he eventually becomes a pious reformer, it is after he has secured his fortune
through smuggling and sharp dealing ("I'd defy the devil in a
trade!"). Cooper maintains throughout his character delineation
the deprecatory tone suggested in his epigraph to one of the
chapters:

> There's Jonathan, that lucky lad,
>   Who knows it from the root, sir;
> He sucks in all that's to be had,
>   And always trades for boot, sir.

Cooper admires Bolt's nautical knowledge and his agility aloft,
but even these virtues cannot now gain for the Yankee reprobate
any better reward than admission to the easiest room in hell.

&ajs; &jea;

From a comic figure in the subplots of the American drama, the Yankee, as Cooper treats him, gradually becomes a stage villain. David Gamut and Joel Strides may derive from the same ancestry, but it is virtually undetectable, so little resemblance do they bear to each other. Although this metamorphosis of the down-East type is clearly a reflection of Cooper's changing relationship with his times, it is justifiable within the framework of the folk tradition. All that one legitimately can require of the artist *as folklorist* is that he project into his works characters whose actions and speech have demonstrable counterparts in oral literature; this Cooper never fails to do. If the features of the Yankee change in his novels, the various profiles that he presents to the reading audience were all recognizable New England faces in nineteenth-century America.

7

◄§ COOPER'S ACHIEVEMENT

COOPER died in 1851 still unreconciled with "the ways of the hour," as he referred to current mores in the title of his last (and unsuccessful) novel in 1850. But his estrangement from America could not obscure its recognition of him as its first great novelist and its most influential literary force, both at home and abroad, to that time. He had been the first to prove that America, despite its relatively brief history and barely established body of writings, already held its own sources of romance, tragedy, heroism, humor, and suspense; and that fiction based on these native materials could sustain itself financially in America and even find an audience in Europe, where Cooper's writings had been not only read but imitated.

The popularity of his books, upon which these achievements depended, was attributable to several factors. Primarily, Cooper's works were the first successful novels that were truly American. When *The Spy* appeared in 1821, it became apparent that what Washington Irving was doing in the short story, what John Greenleaf Whittier was to do in poetry, Cooper was now to accomplish in the full-length fictional work; a literature indigenous to the new republic was being created.

Cooper's most successfully used native material proved to be, not contemporary social conflicts, but America's history of the previous century, especially the years and events surrounding the Revolutionary War. The land and sea stories he set in that era, such as *The Spy, The Pilot*—both of which glorify real American heroes—and *The Last of the Mohicans,* gained immediate critical approval and extensive popular sales.

More important than contemporary recognition to later Cooper readers, however, is the fact that in his choice of material he brought to the printed page, however romantically, two epochs of American life that were soon to disappear forever—the day of the frontier and the day of the sailing ship. And he did this in unique ways, so individual to him that they now underlie his literary stature.

For, first, with his *Leather-Stocking Tales* Cooper created the frontier myth that Americans, fascinated by and guilty about the obliteration of the red man, craved. The *Tales* are the saga of the American Indians futilely resisting civilization as they allied with or warred against the vanguard of white men who trail blazed on the western borders. The legend is made romantic by Cooper's verdant settings, by his solemn "good" Indians and his cruel "bad" ones; by his danger-beset courtships by gentlemanly young men for dainty young ladies; by his dramatic escapes-and-pursuits, ambushes, and traitors' betrayals; and above all, by his Leather-Stocking—the lean, simple, totally good white scout whose shooting eye and careful judgment alike never fail.

But despite some perhaps superficial elements, Cooper infuses the whole Leather-Stocking story with the deep tragedy of the dispossession and final destruction of the Indian, a tragedy that the fate of the solitary white scout both represents and parallels. The red man was lost and the singular class of white man, the frontiersman who preceded American civilization through the forests and across the plains, and then was driven on by it, was also finally lost. It is an elegy for him, for the Indian, for the trees that were felled and the game that was destroyed, and for the way of life peculiar to a rough, untamed world, that is voiced by Natty Bumppo and the *Leather-Stocking Tales.*

If Cooper's function was to paint an irrevocable picture of the drama of the American wilderness, his role as a writer of the sea was equally, and in a different way, prime. For he had many successors but virtually no predecessors in the writing of the nautical novel as it is known today. In Cooper's stories the sea itself, for the first time, plays a dominant role; action takes place not in port but on the water; attention is given to weather conditions, ocean storms and calms; the problems and technicalities of actually running the vessel are detailed; and finally, Cooper, partly reflecting other writers and partly originating, reveals the sailor himself—his language, his respect for the powers and mysteries of the sea, his philosophy and personality. Probably second only to Natty Bumppo among Cooper's memorable characters is his first old sailor, Long Tom Coffin of *The Pilot*. Salty, knowing, at once religious and superstitious, he is the first of a nautical crew individualized by Cooper in his novels of the sea. In nonfiction too Cooper brought attention to American seagoing with his two-volume *The History of the Navy of the United States of America*.

Intertwined with Cooper's achievements as mythmaker and genre founder are the unforgettable characters to whom he gave life. Not only do Leather-Stocking, the Indians, and Long Tom endure; Cooper, in true folklorist tradition, immortalized a score of eighteenth- and nineteenth-century folk types. If Long Tom, the first old salt, is also a Yankee—the New Englander as distinguished from the New Yorker—he is one of Cooper's most likable ones, for he is followed by Yankees who vary from the humorous and inoffensive to the vulgarly aggressive trouble-makers of Cooper's social protest novels. Present too in Cooper's works are the comically pretentious scholar; the gregarious, unattractive newspaper editor; the prosperous landowner; the crude and selfish borderman; the American Negro; and all types of women, from the humble, lonely wife of the sea captain and the tough, hard working wife and mother of the frontier, to the curly-haired daughters of outpost army officers and settlers. Enriching all of these characterizations are Cooper's skill in imitating dialect and his use of the folk proverb.

The least popular portion of Cooper's work remains his body of political and social protest. In both fiction and essay form he first praised democracy, the Jeffersonian type, and then turned on it, protesting its degeneration with the Jackson era into "mobocracy"—a government that seemed to let the popular voice overrule law and individual rights.

But every Cooper novel contains examples of his literary fortes: vivid characterization; an aura of romance diffused through adventure, suspense, or love; a sense of native American humor; and well-drawn landscapes and seascapes. Perhaps William Cullen Bryant spoke for posterity when he predicted at a Cooper memorial gathering in New York City in 1852: "The creations of Cooper's genius . . . may remain to the delight of the nations through another great cycle of centuries. . . ."

8

✑ TRENDS IN COOPER CRITICISM

A DECADE before his death in 1851 Cooper had established the literary reputation which has endured through this century. His fame rose rapidly in the 1820's and 1830's and then leveled off on the high plateau where it has since remained, largely unaffected by the shifting tides of taste. Few writers of his time have been so consistently appreciated by audiences of both the nineteenth and twentieth centuries. Among his contemporaries, Thoreau, Melville, and Whitman were misunderstood and neglected until they were "discovered" by modern readers to receive, finally, America's highest esteem. The opposite reversal of fortune befell many others such as Longfellow, Whittier, Holmes, and Lowell, all highly regarded during their own lifetimes but now seldom accorded a primary place among American writers.

At first it was the native quality of Cooper's work that seemed most praiseworthy. In the search for a national literature, reviewers used "American-ness" as a basic criterion of criticism, and in Cooper's novels they found what they had for so long sought. If his manner of writing was at times derivative, his subject matter was undeniably indigenous. His landscapes were often recognizable frontier scenes; many of his characters, whether individualized or typed, were essentially familiar figures, speaking authen-

120

tically a variety of American dialects; and his themes were based on ideas that informed the life of the new republic.

As American literature came of age and a host of writers were beginning to utilize native materials, the scrutiny of Cooper's readers shifted from content to form. It was the craftsmanship of the novels that was now discussed in innumerable commentaries that ranged all the way from the first scholarly biography, by Thomas Lounsbury, to Lowell's *Fable for Critics,* a genial burlesque of contemporary authors. Critics evaluated his characterization; Parkman and Howells found it inferior to the rest of his work, but a majority recognized the classic features of his principal figures, especially Natty Bumppo, Harvey Birch, and Long Tom Coffin. Clearly these belonged in the portrait gallery of literature's greatest characters. Despite the jesting doggerel in which Lowell wrote, he was none the less sincere in his comparison of Natty Bumppo with two of the best-known personalities in the English novel:

> And Natty won't go to oblivion quicker
> Than Adams the parson or Primrose the vicar.

There is ample evidence that his prose style and plot structure were also closely analyzed. A number of perceptive admirers, both at home and in Europe, imitated his novels, especially the various volumes of the *Leather-Stocking Tales.* No less perceptive were the humorists who wrote parodies of these works, notably William Makepeace Thackeray with his *Stars and Stripes* and Bret Harte with *Muck-a-muck.*

If both of these parodists were good-natured in their laughter at Cooper's expense, Mark Twain, America's leading humorist, definitely was not. The most bitter attack on Cooper as a writer came in Twain's "Fenimore Cooper's Literary Offenses." It is a two-edged weapon that cuts both at Cooper and at the literary judgment of Thomas Lounsbury, Brander Matthews, and Wilkie Collins, three eminent critics who had eulogized Cooper's art. Here, in its way, is another instance of Twain's well-known delight in throwing dead cats into sanctuaries. He lists eighteen supposed "offenses" that Cooper committed in *The Deerslayer,* most of them lapses in probability and peculiarities of style. One of his "rules" governing the first type of offense requires that "the personages in a tale shall be alive, except in the case of corpses, and that always the reader shall be able to tell the corpses from the others." Damning Cooper for his stylistic sins, he prescribes that an author "say what he is proposing to say, not merely come near it." Perhaps the most telling observation that Twain makes concerns the discrepancy between the polished poetic lines in Natty Bumppo's speeches and his semiliterate backwoods dialect. Much of what Twain says can be discounted as the reaction of a realist—a disappointed and, at times, embittered realist—against romanticism at its height in prose fiction; as a whole, his essay cannot be taken seriously, though the humor is at times hilarious.

During the first quarter of the twentieth century the bulk of Cooper scholarship lacked originality, and the commentaries, for the most part, did little more than solemnly reaffirm the importance of Cooper's contribution to the development of American literature. Established securely now in the literary hall of fame, he was almost above criticism, it seemed. The very titles of the volumes in which essays on Cooper appeared often suggested this Olympian position: *American Prose Masters*, by William Crary Brownell; *Gateways to Literature*, by Brander Matthews; *Some Makers of American Literature*, by William Lyon Phelps; and finally, in 1931, *Classic Americans*, by Henry Seidel Canby.

But the late 'Twenties saw a renaissance of Cooper criticism that has continued to the present, resulting in a growing body of fresh and provocative studies. There have been several good source studies of individual novels and a number of excellent biographical essays; those dealing with Cooper's personal, social, and literary backgrounds have added much to our understanding of the man. Cooper's achievement in the realm of sea fiction has also been recognized; just recently published is Thomas Philbrick's monumental work, *James Fenimore Cooper and the Development of American Sea Fiction* (1961). Most of the new surge of interest in Cooper, however, has developed along two main lines: 1) analysis of his social, economic, and political thought and its significance for our time as well as his own; and 2) interpretation of Cooper's art for its symbolic value in depicting the American experience of the eighteenth and early nineteenth centuries.

Drastic changes in the American way of life in the late 1920's and 1930's brought intellectuals to a new seriousness that was reflected in the methodologies of literary criticism. Increasingly the criteria of evaluation were other than the purely artistic, deriving more often from the various disciplines of the social sciences: economics, psychology, sociology, political science, and intellectual history. For all of these disciplines, though perhaps less for psychology than for the others, Cooper's work offered a challenge. What was his view of the good life? What, according to Cooper, were the proper relationships among men and between the individual and society? What were the issues on which Cooper dissented so strongly from the majority opinion, and what, in each case, was the philosophical basis of his dissent? These broad questions and their implications absorbed the interest of some of the most astute observers of the American scene.

Such considerations are patent in the title Robert Spiller gave to his illuminating biography of 1931: *Fenimore Cooper: Critic of His Times*. It was followed in 1933 by John Ross's more abstract monograph, *The Social Criticism of Fenimore Cooper*. Ethel Outland wrote a whole case history of the Three-Mile Point Controversy in *The Effingham Libels on Cooper* . . . (1929), and Dorothy Waples pictured in great detail his political image among his contemporaries in *The Whig Myth of Fenimore Cooper* (1938). Cooper's actual political philosophy was analyzed succinctly by H. L. Mencken in his introduction to a new edition of *The American Democrat* in 1931. It would now appear likely that at least part of the scholarship in this vein was done in response to the invitation made in 1927 by V. L. Parrington in his *Main Currents in American Thought* (Vol. II):

> Cooper was a democrat who criticized the ways of a reputed democracy because of his love for an ideal republic. Too few of his kind have arisen in America; too few who dare to speak their minds unterrified by public opinion. . . . An individualist of the old English breed, he could not be intimidated or coerced in the matter of his rights by any clamor, whether of newspapers or mobs. He had his shortcomings in plenty, both as romancer and critic. . . . Yet the more intimately one comes to know him, the more one comes to respect his honest, manly nature that loved justice and decency more than popularity. His daily life became a long warfare with his fellows, who exacted of him a great price for his idealism, but later generations should love him none the less for the battles he fought. That America has been so tardy in coming to know him as a man and a democrat, as well as a romancer, is a reflection upon its critical acumen.

In the resulting studies attention shifted to Cooper's nonfiction, which was direct and seldom figurative—*The American Democrat, A Letter to His Countrymen,* and *Notions of the Americans*—and to the more propagandistic of his socio-political novels. (In his edition of what purported to be *Representative Selections* Spiller devoted the entire volume to Cooper's critical prose, excusing his bias with the plea that the work of a novelist could not be adequately treated in such a framework; in the same series, however, one finds extensive passages of prose fiction among the selections of other novelists.) Ironically, the classic works such as the *Leather-Stocking Tales, The Spy,* and the sea stories were often made to seem less important than, say, *The Monikins, Home as Found,* and the anti-rent trilogy.

Such has not been the attitude taken by those who have followed the other main line of Cooper criticism, the exploration of Cooper's mythopoeic function. For these critics, Cooper's appeal is in the artistic creations in which he gave image to the unarticulated and, at times, subconscious moods and attitudes Americans held concerning life, especially the frontier life of the country's early days.

D. H. Lawrence was the first critic of stature to speak of Cooper's works in these terms in *Studies in Classic American Literature,* published in 1923. In his slangy, flamboyant manner he discussed the *Leather-Stocking Tales* as a type of wish-fulfillment that struck enough sympathetic chords in the general American psyche to take on the quality of a myth:

> Now let me put aside my impatience at the unreality of this vision, and accept it as a wish-fulfilment vision, a kind of yearning myth. Because it seems to me that the things in Cooper that make one so savage, when one compares them with actuality, are perhaps, when one considers them as presentations of a deep subjective desire, real in their way, and almost prophetic.

Precious, provokingly wrongheaded, and at times in error about factual data, Lawrence's essay has been, nevertheless, highly influential, setting a new trend in Cooper studies. Lucy Lockwood Hazard, adapting Turner's "frontier theory" of American history in *The Frontier in American Literature* (1927), followed Lawrence in examining Cooper's image of the wilderness; much of her chapter on Cooper was devoted to his idealization of Indians and pioneers. The issue of realism *versus* idealism in Cooper's portraiture of the Indian has given rise to a number of subsequent articles and chapters. Among these are two of the twelve chapters in *James Fenimore Cooper: A Re-Evaluation* (1954), a collection of the papers read three years earlier at the Cooper Centennial Celebration at Cooperstown. Notable among the so-called "myth critics" of recent years who have continued, at times, in Lawrence's footsteps have been Henry Nash Smith in *Virgin Land,* R. W. B. Lewis in *The American Adam,* Roy Harvey Pearce in *The Savages of America,* and Richard Chase in *The American Novel and Its Tradition.*

Cooper's writings thus continue, as they have from the first, to interest critics and scholars as well as a multitude of "just for pleasure" readers.

SELECTED BIBLIOGRAPHY

Note: Works currently available in paperbound editions are so indicated at the conclusion of the entry.

COOPER'S CHIEF WORKS

The Spy: A Tale of the Neutral Ground. 2 vols. New York: Wiley & Halsted, 1821. (Paperbound)

The Pioneers; or the Sources of the Susquehanna. 2 vols. New York: Wiley, 1823. (Paperbound)

The Pilot: A Tale of the Sea. 2 vols. New York: Wiley, 1824. [This first edition bears the date *1823* on the title page, but it was not actually published until January of 1824.]

The Last of the Mohicans: A Narrative of 1757. 2 vols. Philadelphia: Carey & Lea, 1826. (Paperbound)

The Prairie: A Tale. 2 vols. Philadelphia: Carey, Lea & Carey, 1827. (Paperbound)

The Red Rover: A Tale. 2 vols. Philadelphia: Carey, Lea & Carey, 1828. (Paperbound)

Notions of the Americans Picked up by a Travelling Bachelor. 2 vols. Philadelphia: Carey, Lea & Carey, 1828.

The Water-Witch; or the Skimmer of the Seas: A Tale. 2 vols. Philadelphia: Carey, Lea & Carey, 1830.

The American Democrat; or Hints on the Social and Civic Relations of the United States of America. Cooperstown: H. & E. Phinney, 1838. (Paperbound)

Homeward Bound; or the Chase: A Tale of the Sea. 2 vols. Philadelphia: Carey, Lea & Blanchard, 1838.

Home As Found. 2 vols. Philadelphia: Lea & Blanchard, 1838. (Paperbound)

The History of the Navy of the United States of America. 2 vols. Philadelphia: Lea & Blanchard, 1839.

The Pathfinder; or the Inland Sea. 2 vols. Philadelphia: Lea & Blanchard, 1840. (Paperbound)

The Deerslayer; or the First Warpath: A Tale. 2 vols. Philadelphia: Lea & Blanchard, 1841. (Paperbound)

Satanstoe; or the Littlepage Manuscripts: A Tale of the Colony. 2 vols. New York: Burgess & Stringer, 1845. (Paperbound)

127

The Crater; or Vulcan's Peak: A Tale of the Pacific. 2 vols. New York: Burgess & Stringer, 1847.

The Sea Lions; or the Lost Sealers. 2 vols. New York: Stringer & Townsend, 1849.

ADDITIONAL WORKS

Precaution: A Novel. 2 vols. New York: A. T. Goodrich, 1820.

Lionel Lincoln; or the Leaguer of Boston. 2 vols. New York: Wiley, 1825.

The Wept of Wish-ton-Wish: A Tale. 2 vols. Philadelphia: Carey, Lea & Carey, 1829.

The Bravo: A Tale. 2 vols. Philadelphia: Carey & Lea, 1831.

Letter of J. Fenimore Cooper to Gen. Lafayette on the Expenditure of the United States of America. Paris: Baudry, 1831.

The Heidenmauer; or the Benedictines: A Legend of the Rhine. 2 vols. Philadelphia: Carey & Lea, 1832.

The Headsman; or the Abbaye des Vignerons: A Tale. 2 vols. Philadelphia: Carey, Lea & Blanchard, 1833.

A Letter to His Countrymen. New York: Wiley, 1834.

The Monikins. Philadelphia: Carey, Lea & Blanchard, 1835.

Sketches of Switzerland. By an American. 2 vols. Philadelphia: Carey, Lea & Blanchard, 1836.

Sketches of Switzerland. By an American. Part Second. 2 vols. Philadelphia: Carey, Lea & Blanchard, 1836.

Gleanings in Europe. By an American. 2 vols. Philadelphia: Carey, Lea & Blanchard, 1837. [The work is devoted to Cooper's experiences in and observations of France.]

Gleanings in Europe: England. By an American. 2 vols. Philadelphia: Carey, Lea & Blanchard, 1837.

Gleanings in Europe: Italy. By an American. 2 vols. Philadelphia: Carey, Lea & Blanchard, 1838.

Mercedes of Castile; or the Voyage to Cathay. 2 vols. Philadelphia: Lea & Blanchard, 1840.

The Two Admirals: A Tale. 2 vols. Philadelphia: Lea & Blanchard, 1842.

The Wing-and-Wing; or Le Feu-Follet: A Tale. Philadelphia: Lea & Blanchard, 1842.

Wyandotte; or the Hutted Knoll: A Tale. 2 vols. Philadelphia: Lea & Blanchard, 1843.

Ned Myers; or a Life Before the Mast, ed. J. Fenimore Cooper. Philadelphia: Lea & Blanchard, 1843.

Afloat and Ashore; or the Adventures of Miles Wallingford. 4 vols. in 2 series. New York: Burgess & Stringer, 1844. [In collected editions of the novels this is usually listed as two separate works, and so bound, one under the title and one under the subtitle.]

The Chainbearer; or the Littlepage Manuscripts. 2 vols. New York: Burgess & Stringer, 1845.

The Redskins; or Indian and Injin. Being the Conclusion of the Littlepage Manuscripts. 2 vols. New York: Burgess & Stringer, 1846.

Lives of Distinguished American Naval Officers. 2 vols. Philadelphia: Carey & Hart, 1846.

Jack Tier; or the Florida Reef. 2 vols. New York: Burgess & Stringer, 1848.

The Oak Openings; or the Bee Hunter. 2 vols. New York: Burgess & Stringer, 1848.

The Ways of the Hour: A Tale. New York: G. P. Putnam, 1850.

COLLECTED EDITIONS OF THE NOVELS

Cooper's Novels. Illustrated by F. O. C. Darley. 32 vols. New York: Townsend, 1859-1861. [Often called the "Darley Edition," this is considered by most scholars to be the most nearly definitive.]

J. Fenimore Cooper's Works. Household Edition. 32 vols. New York: Hurd & Houghton, 1876-1884. [In this edition fifteen of the novels have prefaces written by Cooper's daughter Susan.]

The Works of James Fenimore Cooper. Mohawk Edition. 33 vols. New York: Putnam's, 1895-1900. [This edition includes *Ned Myers.*]

LETTERS

The Letters and Journals of James Fenimore Cooper, ed. James F. Beard. 6 vols. Cambridge: Harvard University Press, 1960-   . [The first four volumes (I-II, 1960; III-IV, 1964) carry the letters through 1844. When complete, the work will supersede *The Correspondence of James Fenimore Cooper.* 2 vols. (New Haven: Yale University Press, 1929), complied by the novelist's grandson James Fenimore Cooper.]

BIBLIOGRAPHY

Spiller, Robert E., and Philip C. Blackburn. *A Descriptive Bibliography of the Writings of James Fenimore Cooper.* New York: Bowker, 1934.

BIOGRAPHY

Boynton, Henry Walcott. *James Fenimore Cooper.* New York: Century, 1931.

Bryant, William Cullen. *Memorial of James Fenimore Cooper.* New York: Putnam's, 1852.

Clavel, Marcel. *Fenimore Cooper: Sa vie et son oeuvre: La jeunesse (1789-1826).* Aix-en-Provence: Imprimerie Universitaire de Provence, 1938.

Clymer, W. Shubrick. *James Fenimore Cooper*. Boston: Small, Maynard, 1900.

Grossman, James. *James Fenimore Cooper*. New York: William Sloane Associates, 1949.

Lounsbury, Thomas R. *James Fenimore Cooper*. Boston: Houghton, Mifflin, 1882. [Until the 1930's this was considered the standard biography.]

Ringe, Donald A. *James Fenimore Cooper*. New York: Twayne, 1962.

Spiller, Robert E. *Fenimore Cooper, Critic of His Times*. New York: Minton, Balch, 1931. [A scholarly but very readable work which views Cooper's life in terms of his political and social thought.]

CRITICAL AND INTERPRETIVE STUDIES

Full-Length Works

Barba, Preston A. *Cooper in Germany*. Bloomington: Indiana University Press, 1914.

Clavel, Marcel. *Fenimore Cooper and His Critics*. Aix-en-Provence: Imprimerie Universitaire de Provence, 1938.

Cunningham, Mary, ed. *James Fenimore Cooper: A Re-Appraisal*. Cooperstown: New York State Historical Association, 1954. [This contains the papers read by twelve scholars at the Cooper Centennial Celebration at Cooperstown in 1951.]

Philbrick, Thomas. *James Fenimore Cooper and the Development of American Sea Fiction*. Cambridge: Harvard University Press, 1961. [This is the first full-length treatment of Cooper's sea novels. Perceptive and thorough, it is a milestone in Cooper scholarship.]

Ross, John F. *The Social Criticism of Fenimore Cooper*. Berkeley: University of California Press, 1933.

Shulenberger, Arvid. *Cooper's Theory of Fiction: His Prefaces and Their Relation to His Novels*. University of Kansas Humanities Studies. Lawrence: University of Kansas Press, 1955.

Walker, Warren S., ed. *Leatherstocking and the Critics*. Chicago: Scott, Foresman, 1965. [Critical articles (*pro* and *con*) on the Leatherstocking Tales from the 1820's to the present.]

Waples, Dorothy. *The Whig Myth of Fenimore Cooper*. New Haven: Yale University Press, 1938.

Articles and Essays — General

Bonner, William H. "Cooper and Captain Kidd," *Modern Language Notes,* LXI (1946), 21–27.

Conrad, Joseph. "Tales of the Sea," *Notes on Life and Letters* (London: Dent, 1921), 53–57.

Cowie, Alexander. "James Fenimore Cooper and the Historical Romance," *The Rise of the American Novel* (New York: American Book, 1951), 115–164.

Gates, W. B. "Cooper's Indebtedness to Shakespeare," *Publications of the Modern Language Association,* LXVII (1952), 716–731.

Hastings, George E. "How Cooper Became a Novelist," *American Literature,* XII (1940), 20–51.

Jones, Howard M. "Prose and Pictures: James Fenimore Cooper," *Tulane Studies in English,* III (1952), 133–154.

Kirk, Russell. "Cooper and the European Puzzle," *College English,* VII (1946), 198–207.

Parrington, Vernon L. "James Fenimore Cooper: Critic," *Main Currents in American Thought,* II (New York: Harcourt, Brace, 1930), 222–237. (Paperbound)

Scudder, Harold H. "Cooper and the Barbary Coast," *Publications of the Modern Language Association,* LXII (1947), 184–192.

————. "What Mr. Cooper Read to His Wife," *Sewanee Review,* XXXVI (1928), 177–194.

Spiller, Robert E. "Cooper's Notes on Language," *American Speech,* IV (1929), 294–300.

Van Doren, Carl. *The American Novel: 1780-1939.* Rev. Ed. (New York: Macmillan, 1940), 21–42.

Walker, Warren S. "Proverbs in the Novels of James Fenimore Cooper," *Midwest Folklore,* III (1953), 99–107.

Whitehill, Walter M. "Cooper as a Naval Historian," *New York History,* XXXV (1954), 468–479.

Winters, Yvor. "Fenimore Cooper, or The Ruins of Time," *Maule's Curse* (Norfolk: New Directions, 1938), 25–50.

Articles and Essays on Individual Works and Series

The Spy

McBride, John. "Cooper's *The Spy* on the French Stage," *University of Tennessee Studies in Humanities,* No. 1 (1956), 35–42.

McDowell, Tremaine. "The Identity of Harvey Birch," *American Literature,* II (1930), 111–120.

Walker, Warren S. "The Prototype of Harvey Birch," *New York History,* XXXVII (1956), 399–413.

The Leatherstocking Tales — Treated Collectively

Clemens, Samuel L. "Fenimore Cooper's Literary Offenses," *North American Review,* CLXI (1895), 1–12. [Frequently reprinted, this is now most readily available in Lynn, Kenneth S., ed. *The Comic Tradition in America: An Anthology of American Humor* (New York: Doubleday, 1958), 328–350. (Paperbound) It is the best known burlesque of the *Tales;* good fun but not to be taken for serious criticism.]

Frederick, John T. "Cooper's Eloquent Indians," *Publications of the Modern Language Association,* LXXXI (1956), 1004–1017.

Lawrence, D. H. "Fenimore Cooper's Leatherstocking Novels," *Studies in Classic American Literature* (New York: Doubleday, 1955), 55–73. (Paperbound) [The original hardcover edition was published by Viking Press in 1923.]

McAleer, John J. "Biblical Analogy in the Leatherstocking Tales," *Nineteenth-Century Fiction,* XVII (1962), 217–235.

Pearce, Roy Harvey. "The Leatherstocking Tales Re-Examined," *South Atlantic Quarterly,* XLVI (1947), 524–536.

Smith, Henry Nash. "Leatherstocking and the Problem of Social Order," *Virgin Land: The American West as Symbol and Myth* (New York: Vintage, 1957), 64–76. (Paperbound) [Originally published in 1950 by Harvard University Press.]

The Prairie

Chase, Richard. "The Significance of Cooper: *The Prairie," The American Novel and Its Tradition* (New York: Doubleday, 1957), 52–65. (Paperbound)

Flanagan, John T. "The Authenticity of Cooper's *The Prairie," Modern Language Quarterly,* II (1941), 99–104.

Muszynska-Wallace, E. Soteris. "The Sources of *The Prairie," American Literature,* XXI (1949), 191–200.

Vandiver, Edward P. "Cooper's *The Prairie* and Shakespeare," *Publications of the Modern Language Association,* LXIX (1954), 1302–1304.

Wasserstrom, William. "Cooper, Freud and the Origins of Culture," *American Imago,* XVII (1960), 423–437.

The Pathfinder

Balzac, Honore de. *Oeuvres Completes,* XXIII (Paris: Calmann-Levy, 1879), 584–592.

The Deerslayer

Davis, David Brion. "The Deerslayer, a Democratic Knight of the Wilderness," *Twelve Original Essays,* ed. Charles Shapiro (Detroit: Wayne State University Press, 1958), 1–22. (Paperbound)

Satanstoe

Chase, Richard. "The Significance of Cooper: *Satanstoe," The American Novel and Its Tradition* (New York: Doubleday, 1957), 47–52. (Paperbound)

Hicks, Granville. "Landlord Cooper and the Anti-Renters," *Antioch Review,* V (1945), 95–109.

The Crater

Gates, W. B. "Cooper's *The Crater* and Two Explorers," *American Literature,* XXIII (1951), 243–246.

———. "A Defense of the Endings of Cooper's *The Crater," Modern Language Notes,* LXX (1955), 347–349.

McCloskey, J. C. "Cooper's Political Views in *The Crater*," *Modern Philology*, LIII (1955), 113–116.

Scudder, Harold H. "Cooper's *The Crater*," *American Literature*, XIX (1947), 109–126.

The Sea Lions

Melville, Herman. "Review of Cooper's *The Sea Lions*," *Literary World*, IV (April 28, 1849), 370.

INDEX

Note: Fictional characters, ships, and other subjects are entered in small capital letters.

Index

Brown, Mrs. James, 15
Brown, William Hill, 20
Brownell, William Crary, 122
Bryant, William Cullen, 43, 91, 119
BUFFALO BILL, 38
BUMPPO, NATTY, 25, 27, 28, 30–44
passim, 49–63 *passim,* 106, 113,
117, 118, 121, 122; ages and various names in the *Leather-Stocking
Tales,* 33
Bunker Hill, 25
Burlington, N. J., 1, 4
Burns, Robert, 22
BUSH, ISHMAEL, 60, 62
Byron, George Gordon, 6th Baron,
25, 40, 65, 73

Cable, George Washington, 37
Calvinists, 111
Cambridge History of American Literature, 44
Canby, Henry Seidel, 122
CAP, CHARLES, 76–7
Cape of Good Hope, 81
Cape Horn, 69
Capri, Italy, 15
Captain Singleton (Defoe), 68, 69
Carey, publishing house, 24
Carson, Kit, 31
Cass, Governor, 46
Cato (Addison), 95
Cervantes Saavedra, Miguel de, 21
Chainbearer, The, 26, 94, 95–7
Chamber of Deputies, France, 18
Charles X, King of France, 16
Charlevoix, 60
Charlotte Temple (Rowson), 20
Chase, Richard, 33, 125
CHINGACHGOOK, 28, 33–7 *passim,*
48–58 *passim,* 62, 63
Christianity, 67
Clark, William, 60
Classic Americans (Canby), 122
Clinton, DeWitt, 14
CLINTON, SIR HENRY, 22
Clintonian Republicans, 11
COEJMANS, ANDRIES, 97
Coffin, Captain Charley, 76
COFFIN, LONG TOM, 65, 75–6, 78, 80,
81, 113, 118, 121
Coffin family, 75
Collins, Wilkie, 121
Columbia University, 14, 84
Columbus, Christopher, 64, 65
COMMODORE, THE, 103
Concord, Mass., 25, 42

Confiscation Act of 1777, 9
Connecticut River, 103
Conrad, Joseph, 64, 67, 70, 74, 75
Cooper, Elizabeth Fenimore, author's
mother, 1, 3, 4, 11; *illus.,* 5
Cooper, James Fenimore:
Biography: Acknowledgment in
America and abroad, 27–9, 116,
120; and Anti-Rent Wars, 94,
99–100; Brothers, 1, 6, 8, 11–12;
Childhood, 1–4; Children, 14,
15, 60, *illus.* 17; Death, 29, 100,
116; European tour, 13–19, 86;
Father, 1–11 *passim,* 88, 89, 104;
Homes, 3, 11, 86, *illus.* 99;
sources for Indians, 46–9, 58–
60; champion of Jeffersonian
democracy, 86–102, 107–8, 118,
123; and Lafayette, 15, 16–19;
Marriage and decade following,
9–10, 11–12; Mother, 1, 3, 4,
11, *illus.* 5; in Navy and later
attachment to it, 6–11, 82–5,
118; Novels, First, 12–13, 116,
Last, 24, 116, Number of, 24;
troubles with Press, 19, 84–5,
89–91; Schooling, 4–6; and
Three-Mile Point Controversy,
89–90; and Yankees, 3, 102–
15, 118; *also see* Chronology,
xiii–v
Compared with: Bryant, 43; Byron, 25, 65, 73; Conrad, 64, 67;
Defoe, 68, 101; Dickens, 14, 42;
Faulkner, 32, 41; Forester, 67;
Hawthorne, 23–4; Heggen, 64;
Hemingway, 41; Holmes, 120;
Irving, 21, 106, 116; Longfellow,
120; Lowell, 120; McFee, 67;
Melville, 67, 79–81, 120; Milton, 60; Parkman, 31–2, 37;
Riesman, 108; Scott, 13, 14, 22,
24, 64, 68, 73, 102; Smollett, 25,
66, 68, 73; Thoreau, 11, 42, 120;
Twain, 41; Whitman, 120;
Whittier, 116, 120; Wordsworth,
3, 43–4
Criticism of, quoted: by Balzac,
28, 32; Bryant, 119; Conrad, 70;
Gardiner, 21; Lawrence, 124;
Lowell, 121; Melville, 66, 70;
Parrington, 123; Twain, 121–22;
Winters, 65
Illustrations: *frontispiece,* 109
Novels classified: 26–7
Cooper, Richard, 8

136

Index

Greeley, Horace, 90
Guide in the Wilderness, A, (William Cooper), 2

HARD-HEART, 61, 62
HAROLD, CHILDE, 69
HARPER, MR., 22
Harte, Bret, 121
HATCHWAY, LIEUTENANT, 73
HAWKEYE, *see* BUMPPO, NATTY
Hawthorne, Nathaniel, 23, 24, 29
Hazard, Lucy Lockwood, 124
Headsman, The, 26, 78, 87
Heathcote family, 9
Heckewelder, the Reverend John, 46–7, 48, 57
Heggen, Thomas, 64
Heidenmauer, The, 26, 87
Helderberg Mountains, 93
Heliodorus of Emesa, 68
Hemingway, Ernest, 41, 78
HEYWARD, MAJOR DUNCAN, 54, 55, 57
Hillhouse, James A., 4
HIST, *see* WAH-TA-WAH
History of the Navy of the United States of America, The, 84–5, 118; *illus.,* 83
Holmes, Oliver Wendell, 120
Home as Found, 26, 44, 87, 88–90, 91, 103, 108–13 *passim,* 124
Homer, 67
Homeward Bound, 26, 66, 68, 69, 71–2, 76, 87, 88, 90, 91–2, 111, 113–14
HORNBLOWER, MR., 101
Howells, William Dean, 121
Hudson, N. Y., 75, 93
Hudson River, 2, 22, 92, 95
Huron Indians, 41, 43, 47, 50–57 *passim*
HUTTER, HETTY, 50
HUTTER, JUDITH, 36, 43, 50, 52
HUTTER, TOM, 50, 53

Indian and Injin, see Redskins, The
Iroquois Indians, 1, 35, 47, 48–9, 52–60 *passim*
Irving, Washington, 21, 106, 116
ISHMAEL, 75, 77, 80

Jack Tier, or, The Florida Reef, 26, 65, 66, 77–8, 100
Jackson, Helen Hunt, 37
Jacksonian democracy, 86, 88, 102, 110, 118

James Fenimore Cooper and the Development of American Sea Fiction (Philbrick), 122
James Fenimore Cooper: A Re-Evalution, 125
Jay family, 4
Jefferson, Thomas, 4, 7
Jeffersonian democracy, 86, 88, 102, 107, 118
Jemison, Mary, 46
Johnson, Captain John, 6, 7
JONATHAN, BROTHER, 104, 114
Jones, John Paul, 65, 67, 82
JUAN, DON, 69
July Revolution of 1830, 16

Kent, James, 14
King, Charles, 14

La Farge, Oliver, 37
Lafayette, Marquis de, 15, 16–18
La Grange, 16
Lake Geneva, 10, 15, 78
Lake George, 33, 54
Lake Ontario, 8, 33, 58
Last of the Mohicans, The, 26, 33, 35, 41, 43, 53–7, 62, 63, 105–6, 117
Lawrence, D. H., 124, 125
Lawrence, James, 8–9
LEATHER-STOCKING, *see* BUMPPO, NATTY
Leather-Stocking Tales, 1, 4, 25, 28, 30–63, 76, 117, 121, 124; *classified,* 33
Le corsaire rouge (Berlioz), 29
LE FEU-FOLLET, 67
"Legends of the Thirteen Republics," 25
Leghorn, Italy, 10, 15
Le National, 18
Lenni Lenape Indians, *see* Delaware Indians
Les Chouans (Balzac), 28
Les Mohicans de Paris (Dumas), 28
Letter from an American Farmer (Crèvecœur), 45
Letter of J. Fenimore Cooper to General Lafayette, 18, 86
Letter to His Countrymen, A, 124
Lewis, Meriwether, 60
Lewis, R. W. B., 125
Lewis Tavern, Albany, N. Y., 9
Lexington, Mass., 25
Lincoln, Abraham, 112
Lionel Lincoln, 25, 26
Literary World, 70

138

Index

Onondaga Indians, 47, 96
O'REGAN, TEAGUE, 21
Original Narratives of Early American History, 46 f.
Osborne, Captain Jonathan, 11
Oswego, N. Y., 8
Otsego County, 2, 7, 11, 40
Otsego Hall, vii, 3; *illus.,* 99
Otsego Lake, vii, 1, 10, 33, 50, 89
Outland, Ethel, 123

Paris, France, 14, 15, 16
Parkman, Francis, 31–2, 37, 47, 121
Parrington, V. L., 123
PATCH, SAM, 104
PATHFINDER, *see* BUMPPO, NATTY
Pathfinder, The, 26, 28, 33, 37, 41, 42, 43, 44, 47, 57–8, 62, 63, 76
Pawnee Indians, 30, 33, 47, 58, 60, 61–2
Pearce, Roy Harvey, 37, 125
Penn, William, 55
PEQUOD, 80, 81
Peregrine Pickle (Smollett), 25, 66, 73
Perry, Commodore Oliver, 84
Perry family, 84
Pershing, John Joseph, 31
PETER COFFIN'S SPOUTER INN, 75
PEYTON, MISS, 105
Phelps, William Lyon, 122
Philadelphia, Pa., 3
Philbrick, Thomas, 122
PICKLE, PEREGRINE, 66
Pilot, The, 13, 25, 26, 28, 65, 67, 71–82 *passim,* 117, 118
Pinkster Festival, 95, 112
Pioneers, The, 13, 25, 26, 33, 36, 37, 38, 58, 62–3, 74, 88, 94; *illus.,* 59
PIPES, BOS'N, 73
Pirate, The (Scott), 13, 68
Pompeii, Italy, 15
Potawatami Indians, 47
Power of Sympathy, The (Brown), 20
Prairie, The, 26, 33, 38, 39, 40, 58–62, 63
PRATT, DEACON ICHABOD, 111, 112
Precaution, 12, 20, 24, 26
Prelude, The (Wordsworth), 43
Pre-Romantics, 45
Primitivism, 45
PRIMROSE, DR., 121
Princeton (College of New Jersey), 6
PUMP, BEN, 74

Quick, Tom, 40
QUIXOTE, DON DE LA MANCHA, 21

RACHEL, 81
Ramona (Jackson), 37
RANDOM, RODERICK, 66
RAVENSNEST, 95, 98
RED ROVER, 67, 71
Red Rover, The, 26, 29, 65, 71, 79
Redskins, The, 26, 27, 94, 96, 97–100
Reformation era, 87
Republican party, France, 16
Republicans, 3
Requiem for a Nun (Faulkner), 32
Revolutionary War, *see* American Revolution
Révue Britannique, 18
Révue Parisienne, 28
Richardson, Samuel, 20
Riche, Barnabe, 67–8
Riesman, David, 108
RIVENOAK, 52
Rives, William, 19
Robinson Crusoe (Defoe), 22, 101
Roderick Random (Smollett), 25, 66, 68, 73
"Romance," 21–2, 25, 117
Rome, Italy, 15
Ross, John F., 123
Rourke, Constance, 105
Rousseau, Jean Jacques, 45
Rowson, Susanna, 20

Sag Harbor, N. Y., 10, 75
St. Peter's Church, Albany, N. Y., 4
SANCHO PANZA, 21
Sand, George, 28
SANTIAGO, 78
SATANSTOE, 95, 112
Satanstoe, 26, 94–5, 107, 111, 112
Savages of America, The (Pearce), 125
Scarlet Letter, The (Hawthorne), 29
Schubert, Franz, 27
Schuyler family, 2, 9, 104
Scott, Sir Walter, 13, 14, 15, 22, 24, 28, 64, 68, 73, 74, 102
Scott, General Winfield, 14
SEA LION, 78
Sea Lions, The, 26, 66, 69–70, 76, 100, 111, 112
Seward, Governor of New York, 93
Shipman family, 40
Shubrick, Commodore William, 10
Simplon Pass, 15

140

3101